RAMBLER'S REWARDS
Cooking from Coast to Coast

RAMBLER'S REWARDS
Cooking from Coast to Coast

Elizabeth Guy & Pat Kirkbride
PHOTOGRAPHY by Derry Brabbs

F

FRANCES LINCOLN LIMITED
PUBLISHERS

CONTENTS

INTRODUCTION

We first got to know each other when we worked at the Wensleydale Creamery in Hawes and our paths have continued to cross ever since. We have turned from colleagues to good friends, sharing a passion for the area in which we live and the food it produces. Family life permitting, we both enjoy a day out shopping – but we're far more likely to get enthusiastic about the fine marbling on a rib of beef in a good butcher's or finding an artisan cheesemaker, than a pair of shoes or the latest handbag.

Over the years, we have both been involved in a variety of food- related businesses and have experienced the dynamic changes in the food and farming industry, as well as food retailing. Farming has been a challenging industry for many decades, particularly for hill farmers facing rising costs, competition from overseas markets and falling prices for their produce year on year. It has been an exciting time to be involved in food, with a definite sea change towards home-grown produce involving fewer food miles to bring it from field to fork. There have been commendable efforts to make people see the benefits of eating seasonal ingredients as well as the joys to be had from producing and cooking your own food.

The idea for this book started to germinate when Doreen Whitehead retired. Doreen is Pat's mother and quite a character. She and her husband Ernest had lived and loved the Coast to Coast walk for over 20 years. Through their farmhouse bed and breakfast, Butt House, which sits on the Coast to Coast at Keld, they had welcomed hundreds of walkers into their home, providing shelter and sustenance, as well as a tale or two.

The connections between our love of food, farming and the landscape, along with the hospitality offered through Doreen and Ernest, were too great to ignore and *Rambler's Rewards: Cooking from Coast to Coast* was born. The book follows a walk through the day – from hearty and healthy breakfasts to lunch at home or on the move, teatime treats and suggestions for supper. Our recipes are either quick and easy to prepare at the end of a busy day or could have been prepared in advance and frozen, refrigerated or left on timer for when you get in. Living in the heart of the country, as we do, we have tried to use ingredients which are readily available wherever you live, without the need for trips to the supermarket or specialist shops.

Our aim is to give recipes that inspire you to plan a great day out as well as to celebrate the glut of wonderful produce available. Although we have selected suppliers from the North of England, from the west coast to the east, we would encourage you to take a closer look at your own locality and find some of the small producers in your own area who are passionately involved in making a difference to the quality of food we consume.

Although our book was inspired by the Coast to Coast walk, with walking and holidaying along the route, the recipes are ideal for our demanding and often chaotic everyday lives. A casserole prepared in the evening to be waiting in the oven after a busy day at work; an economical and healthy bowl of soup for lunch at the office; pizza slice and honey and seed flapjacks for the children's lunch box; a sumptuous cake for a family tea or a quiche, salad and glass of wine to share with friends. There is a recipe for every occasion which we are sure you will find straightforward yet rewarding to make.

So, next time you have an opportunity, why not eat a hearty breakfast, pack up a tempting lunch and head out for the hills to celebrate the best of the British countryside?

Elizabeth Guy and Pat Kirkbride

THE QUEEN OF THE COAST TO COAST

What is the most important part of a successful walking holiday? A comfortable bed, a hot bath and some good food? A first-rate B&B is a gem on any holiday, but, when you're walking long distances, it's an essential.

Doreen Whitehead is an institution in the Dales – probably the best known woman in Wensleydale and Swaledale. Through her many years running a bed and breakfast establishment, her fame has spread to all corners of the United Kingdom and far beyond.

She was born just before the Second World War and moved to a little village near Masham and the safety of her grandparents' farm for the duration of the war. As her father was away fighting and her mother worked assisting births, Doreen spent a lot of time with her grandmother, who she cites as a great influence on her – teaching her to cook and to enjoy the experience of feeding others well. When her father returned after the war, the family stayed in Masham and, after school and college, Doreen started work for British Rail, finding herself at Hawes station, where she was the last clerk before the station was closed down in the late 1950s. She met and married her first husband, Edmund Kirkbride, in 1958 and there began her long association with the Upper Dales. Sadly, Edmund died in 1976.

Over the years, as well as bringing up three children, Doreen worked her way from office administration to catering, starting with the Black Bull Café in Hawes and the Auction Mart Café at the local livestock auction. She also developed a thriving outside catering business serving good wholesome food at weddings, funerals, parties and, most influentially, Muker Show judges' lunches. It was here that she met her second husband, Ernest Whitehead, who she married in 1980 and with whom she started their B&B.

Like many bed and breakfast establishments, particularly ones within working farms, Doreen started it to supplement the income from the farm. She is a shrewd businesswoman who saw that Wainwright's Coast to Coast walk was becoming increasingly popular as a walking holiday and, given the situation of their farm in Keld, in the middle of the route, she realised that they could find some regular guests. Due to the remoteness of the area and lack of local eateries, particularly for walkers, she and Ernest provided an evening meal. When they started in 1984, the charge for a night's accommodation was £5 with £3.50 for dinner. When Ernest reached retirement age in 1996, they sold the farm to the local estate and bought Butt House, a larger house in the village which they renovated to provide en-suite facilities and more rooms.

Doreen was well ahead of her time in her desire to use local produce, particularly meat from the local farms. She recounts one lovely tale about a couple from Beverley who often stayed with them and had requested to have roast beef and Yorkshire pudding for their evening meal. He was delighted that she could tell them from which farm the meat had come. The morning after their meal, the couple had driven off and stopped for lunch at a local pub. He wrote after he returned home to say that when he had asked the waitress if the chicken in their pie was local, she had replied, 'Yes, I think it came from Tesco's.' He remarked that, had Doreen served him chicken and he had asked the same question, she would probably have known it since it was an egg.

Doreen and Ernest stayed at Butt House until 2008 when they decided that the time had come for them both to retire and see the world outside the Dales. They still live in Keld and always have the kettle handy for their many visitors.

BREAKFAST

There is a saying, 'Eat breakfast like a king, lunch like a prince and dinner like a pauper.' It obviously makes sense that you are far more likely to burn off the calories from a big breakfast than from dinner. In addition to the benefits to weight control, you need to have a good start if you are to have an active day. Whether it's a bowl of porridge in winter, fruit, yoghurt and muesli in summer or a full English breakfast at the weekend, breakfast should be enjoyable, nutritious and sustaining, especially if you are on holiday or planning an action-packed day.

When staying in a hotel or B&B, it is such a treat to have everything laid out for you and it is often difficult to choose between what's available. The options for eggs are enough – creamy scrambled eggs with crispy, locally cured bacon; lightly poached free-range eggs on toast; a fried egg nestled in the middle of the full English; or of course a runny yellow-yolked boiled egg with soldiers.

At home, when you have the time, breakfast can be a special feast: perhaps a simple meal on your own with a bowl of cereal, pot of tea and the papers. Equally enjoyable is sitting down with your family over a good fry-up, deciding what to do with the day ahead.

We have put together a selection of ideas for breakfast which will certainly kick the day off in style.

The full English breakfast

What a classic start to the day! Although not many of us start every day with a full English breakfast, it is one of the luxuries you can afford yourself when on holiday. No stay in a B&B is complete without one and it certainly sets you up for a day's walking. The basics of the full English are good bacon, sausage and black pudding with, of course, a free-range egg, tomato, mushrooms and, if you're really naughty, some fried bread.

Doreen Whitehead, our B&B Queen of the Coast to Coast (see page 7), always used produce from Slacks of Cumbria. As you head out of Orton towards Kirkby Stephen, you probably wouldn't even notice a neat little farm tucked under the hill at Raisbeck. However, Newlands Farm has been producing high-quality sausages, air-dried bacon and traditional-recipe black pudding for over 30 years. All their produce is made from locally sourced pigs, often fed on the whey from the cheese production at the Wensleydale creamery in Hawes. They have a reputation for consistently high-quality, award-winning produce which can be relied upon to give the perfect breakfast. Their honey-roast sausages made from honey-roast pork are the ideal all-rounder, satisfying adults and children alike with their undemanding yet flavoursome taste.

It is worth paying the small premium for good-quality bacon and sausage. Inexpensive bacon usually contains a significant amount of water, salts and preservatives. When you put it in the pan or under the grill, it will shrink considerably and leave an unappealing white residue – properly cured bacon will barely shrink and will result in a crispy, irresistible treat. Cheap sausages are very high in fat and low in meat content, having been bulked up with rusk and other unmentionables. When out walking, look for field mushrooms, particularly in the autumn, as they will offer a burst of earthy flavour to your breakfast, as will a gently cooked ripe vine tomato.

Creamy smoked haddock with scrambled eggs   SERVES 4

When Pat was first offered this dish as a birthday breakfast treat some years ago, she thought it sounded a bit odd and would rather have been given the more traditional scrambled egg and smoked salmon. However, she was quickly converted and it is now a regular breakfast dish in her house.

Put the milk, cream, peppercorns and fish in a pan over a medium heat. Bring to the boil and then immediately remove from the heat. Allow to rest in the milk for 5 minutes and then lift the fish out using a slotted spoon.

Flake the fish into a bowl, keeping it in fairly large pieces. Strain the liquid and keep to one side to use in the scrambled egg.

In a large non-stick pan, soften the shallot in the butter. Reduce the heat and add the beaten eggs with three tablespoons of the poaching liquid. Stir continuously with a wooden spoon until the eggs are creamy.

Stir in the fish and serve immediately with a spoon of crème fraîche if required.

220g (8oz) naturally smoked haddock

8 black peppercorns

150ml (¼ pint) milk

150ml (¼ pint) double cream

1 shallot, finely chopped

60g (2oz) butter

8 free-range eggs, beaten and seasoned with freshly ground black pepper

Crème fraîche to spoon on top (optional)

Fleswick Bay near St Bees, Cumbria

Kippers and brown bread

We have featured Fortune's Smokehouse of Whitby on page 17. A good, freshly smoked kipper is a pungent kickstart to the day, especially when served with some homemade wholemeal bread and butter and a pot of Yorkshire tea. You will need one kipper per person. To cook kippers you can grill them with a little butter or as an alternative (and less smelly way!) put them tails up into a tall jug and pour enough boiling water over to completely cover them. Leave them for 10 minutes, drain and serve with a knob of butter.

Eggy bread

Otherwise known as 'soggy mattresses' in Elizabeth's house as a result of the dish served up to her brothers at boarding school in Wales. Good, fresh white bread and well seasoned farmhouse free-range eggs are the key to memorable eggy bread – also serving straight from the pan and not keeping it in a warming oven probably helps.

In a large bowl, whisk the eggs with the milk, salt and pepper. Put the bread into the egg mixture and leave to soak for a minute.

In a frying pan, melt the butter until it is just bubbling. Put the eggy bread into the pan and fry until it is golden brown on both sides.

Serve immediately with tomato ketchup or relish. If serving at teatime, a few sprigs of fresh parsley in the egg mixture is a pleasant extra flavour.

1 free-range egg per person

1 tablespoon of milk

A good grind of black pepper

A pinch of salt

1 slice of bread per person

30g (1oz) butter for the pan

Honeyed baby tomatoes

SERVES 4

This is a recipe that Pat has adapted from her family. Her grandfather always ate his tomatoes with sugar or honey and, as a child, it was a real treat to have tomato and sugar sandwiches. The addition of a spoon of honey can just take the sharp edge off a tomato sauce or soup and this recipe turns an ordinary dish into something a little more special.

In a small non-stick pan, melt the butter over a medium heat. Add the tomatoes and cook until just softening, then pour the honey over. Stir together and then remove the pan from the heat.

30g (1oz) butter

220g (8oz) cherry tomatoes, cut in half

1 tablespoon of runny honey

Fry the bacon as you like it, then remove it from the pan and keep it warm. Fry the bread in the bacon fat until brown on each side.

8 rashers of good-quality British bacon

4 slices of homemade white bread

For each person, put a slice of fried bread on a warm plate, then two slices of the bacon and then top with a spoon of the honeyed tomatoes. Serve immediately.

Quick kedgeree

SERVES 4

This is a good way to use up leftover rice from a meal the night before (although you must make sure it has been stored in a fridge). It is an attractive, tasty start to the day (or equally delicious for supper). If serving for breakfast, poach the fish the night before and store in the fridge with the cooked rice.

Put the eggs on the hob in a pan of water. When the water is boiling, reduce the heat and simmer for 6 minutes to hard boil.

4 eggs

60g (2oz) butter

In a frying pan, melt the butter and add the cooked rice and fish. Season well with a pinch of salt, plenty of black pepper and the cayenne pepper. Stir until warmed through.

220g (8oz) uncooked weight of basmati or long-grain rice

450g (1lb) smoked haddock fillet, poached in water for 5 minutes

1 teaspoon of cayenne pepper

Peel the eggs, cut into quarters and gently stir into the rice with the chopped parsley. Serve immediately.

Salt and black pepper

A good handful of fresh, chopped parsley

Porridge

Porridge has been enjoyed (or not!) for generations and has recently had a surge in popularity due to its health benefits. It is a dish with so many variations – made with skimmed milk but served with cream and demerara sugar, laced with golden syrup or enriched with sugar and butter. Elizabeth's daughter Emily once accepted an offer of porridge when staying with her great-aunt. She enthusiastically tucked in and spat it straight out – it was made with water and lots of salt. Each to his own.

Porridge is an excellent start to the day if you are walking as it releases energy into the bloodstream steadily through the morning. The type of oats you buy will dictate how quickly the oats cook – the finer the rolled oat the faster it will cook – but they all have the same nutritional content. They are high in calcium, are said to help fight heart disease and aid digestion. If you use a mix of finer, rolled porridge oats with jumbo organic rolled oats you get the speed and creamy texture with a bit of bite from the larger oats.

Honey, seeds and nuts breakfast topper

Nuts are naturally packed with vitamins and essential oils and give a great, slow-release energy boost. You can add alternative nuts or dried fruits to this recipe, or miss out ones you don't like. Pat makes it to stir into porridge but it would be equally delicious with other breakfast cereals or yoghurt and fresh fruit.

Mix the nuts and seeds together and put into a glass jar (screw-top or Kilner). Pour the honey over and allow to sink through the nuts. Stir if necessary to ensure they are all coated.

Spoon over cereal or yoghurt as required.

220g (8oz) mixed nuts (brazils, cashews, almonds, hazelnuts and walnuts)

1 tablespoon each of sunflower, pumpkin and sesame seeds

Half a 340g (12oz) jar of runny honey

Fresh fruit salad

SERVES 4

Fresh fruit is a refreshing and healthy way to start the day. In winter particularly, when oranges are so juicy and succulent, the vitamin C boost will give you a lift and set you up. We have given a citrus salad here which can be prepared the night before, but, if you don't like grapefruit for example, a pineapple would work really well. Just adapt it to suit your preferences.

Peel and segment the fruits, removing all the pips and pith. Squeeze the juice out of the fibrous fruit pieces.

As an added extra refreshing flavour, sprinkle lightly with freshly chopped mint.

1 grapefruit

1 pink grapefruit

2 oranges

Muesli

Make your own muesli – it is so much cheaper than buying it and you get to decide what goes in it. Elizabeth loves dried bananas and apricots as a snack but hates them in cereals as they make everything taste of banana and apricot! Try mixing 220g (8oz) porridge oats and 220g (8oz) jumbo organic oats with 60g (2oz) wheat bran as a base. From there, add 30g (1oz) each of sunflower, sesame and pumpkin seeds; a handful of whole hazelnuts; a handful of flaked almonds and 110g (4oz) raisins. You can tailor the cereal to your own tastes.

Granola

This recipe came from Helen Dalton who runs Holmedale, an excellent B&B in Askrigg, with her husband Ben. She makes everything herself and this is one of her offerings for breakfast. It is great with fruit, yoghurt or simply with milk.

Preheat the oven to 170°C. In a large bowl, thoroughly mix all the ingredients except the raisins using your hands – this keeps the clusters together and gives a crunchier cereal.

Spread the mixture out on to two large baking tins and put in the oven for 40 minutes, turning halfway through the cooking time.

Allow to cool completely – the mixture will crisp up as it cools – and add the raisins. Store in an airtight container.

As an alternative, Helen suggests you try pecan toffee granola. When making the apple sauce, stir in 60g (2oz) of original toffee and replace the almonds with pecans.

450g (1lb) jumbo rolled oats

110g (4oz) sunflower seeds

110g (4oz) white sesame seeds

170g (6oz) apple sauce

2 teaspoons of ground cinnamon

1 teaspoon of ground ginger

110g (4oz) golden syrup

3 tablespoons of runny honey

110g (4oz) light muscovado sugar

220g (8oz) whole almonds

1 teaspoon of Maldon sea salt

2 tablespoons of sunflower oil

280g (10oz) jumbo raisins

FORTUNE'S SMOKEHOUSE

Opposite: Barry Brown transferring the day's smoked kippers from smokehouse to shop

Left: Fortune's Smokehouse shop interior

Whitby's skyline is dominated by the ruins of St Hilda's Abbey, high on Whitby's East Cliff. Spreading below the abbey is a maze of alleyways and narrow streets running down to the harbour. One such street is the cobbled Henrietta Street, halfway up which you will find Fortune's Smokehouse and shop. You could be forgiven for thinking you had stepped back in time as the quaint houses surrounding the shop look much as they would have when it was established by Mr Fortune in 1872. The smokehouse, which has been rebuilt a few times due to a hazard of the trade – catching fire, is next to the shop. However, the smokehouse and method of production remains the same today as it did originally.

The business is now run by brothers Barry and Derek Brown, nephews of the great-great-grandson of the original Mr Fortune. The shop itself is very basic with a display fridge full of kippers, a pile of greaseproof and newspapers to wrap them in, some evocative sepia photographs depicting the Fortune family history which look as if they have been there for ever, and very little else. There are no airs and graces or nods to modern marketing methods here. Fortune's is the only remaining smokehouse in Whitby whereas 100 years ago there would have been a thriving trade. There must have been times when modernisation and diversification were tempting but Barry believes Fortune's has survived because it has stayed true to the fish on which it was founded.

Kippers are smoked herrings, a fish which has been taken from the North Sea for centuries and remains one of our indigenous and sustainable fish today. The health benefits of oily fish are well documented. The fish are hung in rows on rods over natural, untreated oak and beechwood chippings.They are smoked for around 18 hours and once the day's supply is sold, Barry and Derek close the shop – you can't get fresher than that! As the fish are naturally smoked there are none of the additives, preservatives or colourings often found in cheaper, plastic-wrapped offerings.

Elizabeth loves kippers but knows she has eaten one for many hours afterwards – Barry suggests the old method of preventing indigestion is to eat bread and jam afterwards. When we asked him for any recipes he may have, he made it clear that kippers are at their best when left alone – although he did concede that they do make a good pâté. They make a delicious breakfast dish and a quick and easy lunch or supper.

BREADS

There is nothing quite like fresh, homemade bread. It is so much more economical than bought bread but, more importantly, you can control the levels of salt and fat you are eating. When you get the hang of bread making, you can start to be more adventurous with your ingredients, adding herbs, nuts, seeds and different oils. You need to use strong flour which has a higher level of gluten than ordinary flour and gives greater elasticity.

The basic principles of bread making are the same whatever the flour or fat you are using. You need to mix the flours, fat, warm liquid and yeast together and let it rise. Then it needs 'knocking back', which is just knocking the air out of the dough after it has risen, giving it a more even texture. Finally it needs shaping and leaving to rise for a second time (proving) before baking.

Kneading is working the dough to increase the elasticity in the gluten and enable it to rise well and evenly. You can use a Kenwood mixer with a dough hook to do this but it is a fairly easy process and can be quite therapeutic if you need to let off steam. To knead the dough, tip the mixture out on to a clean, well-floured surface or board. Sprinkle a little flour on to the top of the dough and pull the dough from the far outer edge over towards the side nearest to you. As you pull it over, push the base of your palms down on to the top of the dough. Now pick it up and move it round by a quarter turn. Repeat the process until you have a smooth, pliable dough, which will take about 5 minutes. Put the dough back into the bowl and cover with a clean tea towel. Leave for about an hour at warm room temperature until it has doubled in size. You need to 'knock back' the dough after the first rise to remove any larger air bubbles and give a finer texture to the finished bread. Do this by lightly kneading the risen dough until it is smooth and pliable again.

Everyday bread —
white, wholemeal or granary

MAKES 2 LOAVES

You can do this bread in two oiled loaf tins or you can just shape them into an oval and put them on a baking sheet. They are very little effort to make and will keep for at least a couple of days in a bread bin. All bread freezes well so you could have a batch bake while the oven is on and freeze it until it is needed – just take it out the night before and you'll have as-good-as-fresh bread for breakfast.

Put the flour, yeast, oil and salt into a large mixing bowl. Pour half of the warm water into the bowl with the flour and start to mix together with a wooden spoon. Add more water as needed until you have a soft but not sticky dough.

Turn it out on to a clean, well-floured surface. Knead the dough, let it rise and then knock it back in the way described in the introduction to bread on page 18.

Preheat the oven to 200°C. Divide the dough into two. The bottom of the dough (on the floured surface) will become the top of the loaf and you want it to be smooth. To achieve this gently bring the sides of the dough over into the middle as if kneading until you have a smooth underside. Pick the loaf up, turn it over and place the uneven side in the bottom of the tin or on to the baking sheet.

Bake in the middle of the oven for about 25 minutes until well risen and golden brown on top. When you lift the loaf up and tap on the bottom, it will sound hollow if it is cooked through. Place on a cooling rack.

For pizza dough, make in the same way except add 2 tablespoons of olive oil instead of the vegetable oil and make the dough a little more sticky than for bread.

750g (1½lb) strong white, wholemeal or granary bread flour

1 x 7g sachet of fast-action bread yeast or fresh yeast

1 tablespoon of vegetable oil

1 teaspoon of salt

Approximately 450ml (¾ pint) warm water

Milk loaf

Milk loaf is delicious still warm from the oven spread with butter, homemade jam and even a spoon of thick cream. Elizabeth's Cornish granny used to serve her cream teas on 'splits' which were little pillowy buns of milky bread. Make into buns and sprinkle with poppy or sesame seeds or leave as a loaf for slicing.

Put the flour, yeast, butter and salt into a large mixing bowl. Heat the milk until it is warm and then pour into the bowl with the flour. With a wooden spoon mix the milk into the flour and slowly add warm water until you have a soft but not sticky dough.

Turn the dough out on to a clean, well-floured surface. Knead the dough, let it rise and then knock it back in the way described in the introduction to bread on page 18. If making into loaves, divide the dough in two and shape them into an oval. If making buns, divide the dough into 12 evenly sized pieces and shape each one as required.

To make plain buns, take the dough and bring the edges over to give a smooth base, pinch the edges together and then turn the bun over so that the lightly floured underside becomes the top. To make knots, form a sausage shape about 10cm long by rubbing the dough between your hands. Wrap the sausage into a circle and push one end up through the ring as if tying a knot. For plaits, make three small sausages, stick the ends together using milk and plait by crossing over each other. Fold the ends under to give a tidy finish.

For both the buns and loaves, place on a baking sheet lined with parchment paper, cover with a tea towel and leave for about 20 minutes until they have risen again. Take the tea towel off, brush with milk or beaten egg, make three light cuts across the top of the loaves or sprinkle the buns with poppy or sesame seeds and bake in the middle of the oven for about 20 minutes until well risen and golden brown. It is baked through if it sounds hollow when you tap on the bottom of the loaf. Place on a cooling rack.

750g (1½lb) strong white bread flour

1 x 7g sachet of fast-action bread yeast or fresh yeast

60g (2oz) butter

1 teaspoon of salt

300ml (½ pint) full-cream milk

Approximately 150ml (¼ pint) warm water

Poppy and sesame seeds

SALKELD WATER MILL

Thirty-five years ago Nick and Ana Jones were fresh out of university and art college and dreaming of finding a smallholding to grow organic food, milk goats and make bread. Although they were already grinding wheat by hand in a useful wedding present – a coffee grinder – they had not thought of looking for, let alone running, a 250-year-old Cumbrian water mill. However, Nick's arm was getting tired, so when they came across a mill for sale in the Eden Valley, they decided to go for it, much to the consternation of friends and family. They've been milling ever since, and have a national reputation as specialist millers of high-quality organic and biodynamic stoneground flours and cereals.

It feels like stepping back in time watching the mill working. Stone grinding was designed to mill wholegrain flour, which is best for you. The whole grain is ground in one pass between two horizontal, round millstones. The bottom stone, called the bedstone, is stationary and the top stone, the runner, rotates. The grain is fed through a hole in the centre of the stone, the eye. It is ground into flour as it is gradually moved outward between the two stones. These are set very close together, and cut with grooves. In its whole state grain contains a natural balance of starch, protein, vitamins and fibre. In wheat, many oils and essential B and E vitamins are concentrated in the wheat germ. It cannot be separated out in stone grinding which gives the flour its characteristic nutty flavour. Nothing is taken away in the process – whole grain goes in and wholegrain flour comes out. It is slow, simple and labour intensive, so works best on a small scale, at local level, especially where there is a good supply of grain, together with energy, like water or wind.

Given the growing awareness of the challenge and opportunity arising from climate change and the likely reduction in both oil and water supplies worldwide, Nick and Ana are now looking at how to reduce food miles from both ends by sourcing more raw materials locally and supplying more customers in Cumbria. They hope to see more specialist grains grown for them in the north within the next few years. On the energy front they are planting more trees, using local wood for heating and installing a small scale hydro system. It seems ironic that, even though the water mill is using ancient methods of production, it is now seen as a sustainable way to move forward. In addition to selling their flours, Nick and Ana produce a wide range and variety of breads using 12 different flours, including wheat, barley, rye, spelt and oats. Using such pure flour gives a far superior loaf in terms of texture, taste and the power to keep you full enough to walk all day.

Over the years, Ana and Nick have had to look at diverse ways of keeping their business profitable. As such they have developed an award-winning vegetarian tearoom which uses organic ingredients from their own smallholding and local area. They also have a mill shop and gallery to both inform and supply interested customers. In line with the rise of farmers' markets and increasing interest in the origins of our food, Ana teaches popular bread-making and vegetarian cooking courses for both adults and children.

You can combine visiting the mill with beautiful walks up to Long Meg stone circle and along the River Eden. The Settle to Carlisle railway line is nearby and the mill is on the Coast to Coast cycle route.

Sundried tomato and olive bread

This is a lovely bread to serve alongside lasagne or pasta dishes. It also makes a good base for bruschetta-style nibbles before dinner. As you knead the dough, the sundried tomatoes and olives start to break down and infuse the bread with flavour.

Put the flour, yeast, oil, salt, olives, herbs and tomatoes into a large mixing bowl. Put half of the warm water into the bowl and start to mix into the flour. Continue to add the warm water until you have a soft but not sticky dough.

Turn the dough out on to a clean, well-floured surface. Knead the dough, let it rise and then knock it back in the way described in the introduction to bread on page 18.

Preheat the oven to 200°C. Divide the dough into two and work each one either into a round-shaped loaf or a long wide flat loaf shape like a ciabatta.

Bake in the oven for 15 minutes for a long thin loaf or about 25 minutes for a round loaf.

750g (1½lb) strong white bread flour

1 x 7g sachet of fast-action bread yeast or fresh yeast

2 tablespoons of olive oil

2 teaspoons of salt

100g (3oz) pitted olives, black or green, cut into quarters

150g (5oz) sundried tomatoes, finely chopped or pureed

Approximately 450ml (¾ pint) warm water

Either a few sprigs of fresh thyme or 2 teaspoons of dried herbs

Sunrise over the North York Moors from the Vale of Mowbray

Hot cross buns

Good Friday just wouldn't be the same without hot cross buns: served warm with a little butter, these won't stay on the plate for long. This recipe uses a rich dough, similar to milk loaf but with an egg and plenty of spice, but you can cut down the spice according to your own tastes. At any other time of the year, just make spiced buns, missing off the cross, or make the dough into two rich tea loaves.

Put the flour, yeast, butter, egg, spice, dried fruit and sugar into a large mixing bowl. Heat the milk until it is warm and then pour into the bowl with the flour. With a wooden spoon mix the milk into the flour and slowly add warm water until you have a soft but not sticky dough.

750g (1½lb) strong white bread flour (or half white, half wholemeal)

1 x 7g sachet of fast-action bread yeast or fresh yeast

Turn the dough out on to a clean, well-floured surface. Knead the dough, let it rise and then knock it back in the way described in the introduction to bread on page 18.

60g (2oz) butter

1 egg

To make the buns, divide the dough into 12 evenly sized pieces and shape each one into a round by bringing the edges over into the middle to give a smooth underside. Turn the bun over so that the lightly floured side becomes the top. Arrange the buns on a flat baking sheet lined with parchment paper. They do not want to be touching but should be close together. Cover with a tea towel and leave to rise for about 20 minutes.

2 teaspoons of mixed spice

340g (12oz) mixed dried fruit

1 tablespoon of sugar

300ml (½ pint) full-cream milk

To make the cross, put a couple of tablespoons of plain flour in a bowl and mix with cold water to make a thick, gluey paste. Put the paste into a piping bag and, just before putting the buns in the oven, pipe the paste evenly across the tops in one direction and then in the other, making a cross on each one.

Approximately 150ml (¼ pint) warm water

Flour paste to decorate

2 tablespoons of sugar to glaze

Bake in the oven at 190°C for about 20 minutes until golden brown and well risen.

While they are baking, make the sugar glaze by melting the sugar in 6 tablespoons of water and boiling for a minute to thicken slightly but not darken. Remove the buns from the oven and brush with the sugar syrup to glaze.

Allow to cool for about 10 minutes and then serve warm with butter.

Chelsea buns

These buns are perfect when served warm over coffee with friends. They are simple to make but look as if they were a lot more complicated.

Put the flour, yeast, white sugar and 30g of butter in a large mixing bowl. Put half of the warm water into the bowl and start to mix into the flour. Continue to add the warm water until you have a soft but not sticky dough.

Turn the dough out on to a clean, well-floured surface. Knead the dough, let it rise and then knock it back in the way described in the introduction to bread on page 18.

Preheat the oven to 180°C. Oil a 10-inch non-stick round spring-clip tin. On the floured surface, roll the dough out into a 36cm x 25cm rectangle. Using a pastry brush, cover the surface of the dough with the melted butter. Sprinkle with demerara sugar and then the dried fruit.

Now, starting with the side closest to you, carefully roll the dough over like a Swiss roll, finishing with the end on the bottom. Using a sharp knife, cut the long roll into eight equally sized pieces and place them, swirl side up, in the tin, leaving a small gap between each one to allow them to expand. Cover with a tea towel and leave for about 20 minutes to rise.

Bake in the oven for about 25 minutes until golden brown and well risen. Leave the buns to cool in the tin for about 10 minutes and then unclip the tin, brush lightly with melted butter, sprinkle with sugar and serve immediately.

450g (1lb) strong white bread flour

1 x 7g sachet of fast-action bread yeast

1 tablespoon of white sugar

30g (1oz) butter

Approximately 300ml (½ pint) warm water

30g (1oz) melted butter

110g (4oz) mixed dried fruit

30g (1oz) demerara sugar

Melted butter and granulated sugar to decorate

MARCUS CORDINGLEY YORKSHIRE HONEY

Walking along the Coast to Coast route, it can be seen that a significant part of it is covered by moorland heather. At a glance, it may appear quite barren and unproductive, particularly when compared to the lush grassland in between. However, if you are fortunate enough to enjoy lunch on a sunny day on the North York Moors, lie back in the warmth on the spongy bed of heather, close your eyes and you may just hear the gentle, seemingly lazy drone of the honey bees hard at work.

Pat wasn't so lucky with the weather when she took herself off to Scampston to meet well-known beekeeper Marcus Cordingley, but it didn't affect her enjoyment of the day. She has always had an interest in, and an awareness of, the importance of the bee in our fragile ecosystem and had been concerned about reports of serious problems within the industry. Talking with Marcus, he believes the main problems stem from the changes in farming practice over the past few decades. The move to large-scale farming and huge, single-crop fields has led to a massive reduction in the diversity of flora in our landscape. Another factor is the timing of the harvests, particularly the long gap between oil-seed rape flowering and heather coming into bloom. Add to this the lack of hay meadows with their traditional mix of wild flowers and you can see why the bees are struggling to find pollen. The situation is not helped by unseasonably wet and chilly summers, in which the bees are unable to thrive.

Inspecting hives placed on the North York Moors to produce heather honey

For years honey was the only form of natural sweetness and bee keeping has been around for centuries. It's been in the Cordingley family since the early 1950s and Marcus took over the hives from his father, Francis. All 250 hives are within Yorkshire, on fields and the moors.

Bees gather honey from the flowers and store it in the wax combs, which they make themselves, in the hives. They seal the honey with more wax when they have evaporated the moisture. You uncap the honeycomb with a hot knife and remove the honey by centrifugal force in an extractor. It is then filtered and stored before being put into jars. The comb is returned to the hives for the bees to use again.

It seems ironic that there has to be a Best Before date on a product that will last for ever. Although the structure of the honey may change over time, it is self-purifying and always edible. The health benefits of honey are well documented and it is used in many natural healing remedies. Marcus's family eat a jar a week and he claims that none of his four children are ever off school with a cold – it was even recommended by the vet as a possible treatment for Elizabeth's Labrador's allergy to grass. It is claimed to be a natural energy booster and, conversely, you can stir it into milk for a natural sedative.

It is frequently used as a natural sweetener in baking (see honey and seed flapjack, page 85), stirred into cherry tomatoes for a deliciously different accompaniment to bacon or ham and is unbeatable drizzled over the top of good natural yoghurt with fruits for breakfast. Or simply enjoy it on hot buttered toast.

LUNCH

You've made the effort to go for a walk – the least you deserve is a decent lunch. Whether it be on a hill top – 'lunch with a view' – by a river, back at the house or in a tearoom, it should be enjoyable and, hopefully, memorable.

In a perfect world, you get out the checked tablecloth and spread it on the ground for an outdoor banquet. In reality, you are more likely sheltering behind a wall from the rain and shouting to each other through the wind. 'Bring and share' is best, where you arrange in advance who is going to bring what and put it all in the middle for everyone to enjoy. That way, you get to try some foods you may not usually cook for yourself and can do one dish of a decent size instead of bits and pieces for one.

In this chapter, we have put together soups for cold weather, pastries and pizzas for sustenance and delicious light lunches both for on the move, at home or even in the office. Many of the recipes in this section can double up as starters for a main meal – particularly the Wensleydale mushrooms, pâtés, soups and risottos.

Sausage plait

SERVES 6

This is really just a big sausage roll made to look impressive with a bit of rolling and cutting. The recipe here is for a plain sausage plait, but you can make it more special by adding chunks of blue cheese or tomatoes, herbs, mushrooms – whatever suits the people you are feeding. Just add to the sausage meat at the same time as the onion.

Preheat the oven to 200°C. Roll out the pastry into a rectangle about 30cm x 20cm.

Put the sausage meat in a bowl. In a pan, soften the onion in the butter and add to the bowl, mixing well. Put the sausage mixture down the middle of the long length of the pastry.

With a sharp knife, cut slits 3cm apart, 1cm away from the meat, to the edge of the pastry, slanting away from you. Brush with beaten egg. Starting at the end nearest to you, fold the pastry cuts alternately over each other, to give a 'plait' effect. Brush again with the egg.

Transfer to a baking tray and bake in the centre of the oven for 15 minutes. Reduce the temperature to 160°C and bake for a further 20 minutes until golden brown, well risen and bubbling at the sides.

If at home, serve warm with tomatoes and a green salad or baked beans and new potatoes. If eating outdoors, slice into pieces and wrap in tinfoil.

Half a 500g (1lb) packet of chilled puff pastry

750g (1½lb) good sausage meat

1 small onion, diced

15g (½oz) butter

1 egg, beaten

Vegetarian plait

Preheat the oven to 200°C. Roll out the pastry into a rectangle about 30cm x 20cm.

Put the peppers, red onion and garlic on a baking tray with the pinenuts. Sprinkle with olive oil and toss with your hands to coat the vegetables. Bake in the oven for 20 minutes until softened and lightly browned.

Put the cooked vegetables with the cheese evenly down the middle of the pastry. Scatter with small sprigs of thyme. With a sharp knife, cut slits 3cm apart, 1cm away from the vegetable mixture to the edge of the pastry, slanting away from you. Brush with beaten egg. Starting at the end nearest to you, fold the pastry cuts alternately over each other, to give a 'plait' effect. Brush with the egg.

Transfer to a baking tray and bake in the centre of the oven for 15 minutes. Reduce the temperature to 160°C and bake for a further 20 minutes until golden brown and well risen.

If at home, serve warm with couscous and a green salad. If eating outdoors, wrap whole in tinfoil and slice when ready to eat.

Half a 500g (1lb) packet of chilled puff pastry

2 red peppers, deseeded and sliced

1 orange pepper, deseeded and sliced

1 yellow pepper, deseeded and sliced

1 medium red onion, finely diced

2 cloves of garlic, finely diced

60g (2oz) pinenuts

2 tablespoons of olive oil

110g (4oz) soft goat's cheese, sliced, or chunks of feta cheese

Small bunch of fresh thyme

1 egg, beaten

Vegetarian plait before folding the pastry

Pork pie

Homemade pork pie is so delicious and you know there are none of the preservatives and colourings that are often added to commercial pies. When ordering the mince for this pie, ask the butcher to run some bacon through the mincer with the pork, to give a bit of colour and texture. You can make it in a 25cm round, loose-bottomed cake tin or a tray bake tin and cut it into squares: the quantities needed are the same. For a classic old-fashioned, pub-type meal, serve hot with mashed potato, mushy peas and gravy or serve cold as part of a picnic or buffet.

Put the flour, butter, lard and salt in a bowl and mix together until it resembles fine breadcrumbs. Add the egg and slowly add the water until the mixture comes together to form a ball. Put the pastry on to a floured surface and cut so that you have one-third and two-thirds.

Using the larger piece first, roll out until it is large enough to line the base and sides of the tin. Carefully lift the pastry over the well-oiled tin and press down into the base, without tearing the pastry (if you do tear it, patch it using a bit of spare pastry and a little egg to make it stick). Roll out the remaining pastry into a piece just large enough to cover the top of the pie. Keep to one side whilst you make the filling.

To make the filling, simply put all the ingredients in a bowl and mix together thoroughly. Put into the pastry-lined tin and press down firmly and evenly. Brush the sides of the pastry with beaten egg. Roll out the remaining pastry to fit the top of the pie. Place on top and press firmly into the sides to seal and, using a sharp knife, cut around the top of the tin. Brush the top with beaten egg to glaze. Cut a small slit in the middle of the pie and a few around the top, to allow any air to escape while cooking.

Decorate the top with leaves cut from any spare pastry. Brush the leaves with egg. Bake in the oven at 200°C for 20 minutes and then reduce the temperature to 170°C and bake for a further 45 minutes until golden brown and bubbling slightly through the slits on the top.

If serving as a buffet pie, leave it to cool in the tin and then take a sharp knife and cut around the edge. Carefully ease the pie away from the sides of the tin. If serving hot, eat immediately, although it will keep its heat well for a good half hour.

FOR THE PASTRY

340g (12oz) plain flour

110g (4oz) butter

85g (3oz) lard

A pinch of salt

A yolk of an egg

Cold water

FOR THE FILLING

1kg (2.2lb) minced pork

4 slices of bread, made into breadcrumbs

1 teaspoon of salt

A good grind of black pepper

Half a teaspoon of freshly ground nutmeg

Chicken and ham pie

This pie is made in exactly the same way as for pork pie, just the filling differs. It is certainly a pie for eating cold as part of a buffet or picnic – not one for mushy peas and mash. We have specified chicken breasts for this recipe but you could use up leftover roast chicken if you have some.

As for pork pie, simply put all the ingredients in a bowl and mix together thoroughly. Finish off and cook the pie in the same way as on page 33.

FOR THE FILLING

3 chicken breasts, cut into chunks

340g (12oz) cooked ham, cut into chunks

450g (1lb) sausage meat

A good handful of parsley

1 egg

Game pie

We are very fortunate that we live in the midst of some of the best grouse moors in the country, so grouse, pheasant and partridge are plentiful in season. There is also no shortage of plump, succulent rabbits. Since all game is relatively expensive, it is worth spending a bit of time making a good game pie, as it really is a treat.

Put all the game meat with the other ingredients in a large bowl and leave to marinate overnight.

The following day, drain off any excess liquid and remove the bay leaves and juniper berries. Add the sausage meat to the game mixture and combine thoroughly. This helps to keep the meat together in the pie, but also keeps it moist.

Make the pie in the same way as pork pie but, after the first 30 minutes, cover with tinfoil to prevent it browning any further, reduce the oven temperature to 160°C and cook for a further hour.

It can be served hot with spiced red cabbage and mashed potato with a good strong gravy (made using the marinating liquor) or served cold as a magnificent centrepiece to a buffet.

1kg (2.2lb) mixed game meat – any combination will do

220g (8oz) sausage meat

1 medium onion, finely diced

A small handful of crushed juniper berries

3 bay leaves

4 sprigs of thyme, chopped

A good few grinds of black pepper and about ½ teaspoon of salt

Half a bottle of good red wine

Egg and bacon pie

This pie evokes memories of being in the hayfield at teatime during harvest – all sitting round on bales, hot and tired, tucking into a well-deserved spread of proper country food, refreshed with homemade lemonade. It is made even more special with naturally yellow-yolked, free-range eggs and some good local dry-cured bacon.

Preheat the oven to 180°C. You will need a well-buttered, traditional pie dish, about 25cm in diameter.

Make the pastry by mixing the flour, salt and fats together until they resemble fine breadcrumbs and adding enough cold water to bring it all together into a ball. Roll out just over half of the pastry until it is big enough to line the bottom of the pie dish, letting it fall just over the edge of the dish.

In a frying pan, fry off the pieces of bacon until they are cooked and browning slightly. Drain off any excess liquid.

Arrange half of the bacon pieces on the bottom of the pie dish. Crack 4 of the eggs into a bowl, with the parsley, a pinch of salt and a good grind of black pepper and whisk thoroughly. Pour on to the bacon. Now carefully crack the remaining 8 eggs evenly into the pie dish on top of the egg mixture, keeping them whole if possible. Grind black pepper over the eggs and arrange the rest of the bacon slices on top.

Roll out the remaining pastry and use to cover the pie. Press down firmly at the edges. Gently brush with beaten egg and make a few small slits through the pastry top, to allow the pie to expand as it cooks.

Bake in the oven for 45 minutes until golden brown and firm to the touch. Allow to cool for about 15 minutes before serving or eat cold.

FOR THE PASTRY

340g (12oz) plain flour

85g (3oz) butter

85g (3oz) lard

A pinch of salt

Cold water

FOR THE FILLING

16 slices of back bacon, cut into small pieces about 1cm wide

12 eggs

A handful of fresh parsley, chopped

Salt and black pepper

Cornish pasties

Elizabeth's mother is Cornish and her granny still lives in Polperro. Her mother has wonderful stories of her childhood which sound like something straight out of an Enid Blyton book. At weekends in summer all the families would get together and go off in boats to little coves only accessed via the sea. The children would play and explore on the rocks, the women gossip and set up the communal picnic and the men fish for mackerel to grill on an open fire. Cornish pasties were a staple on such occasions.

Put the flour, suet and salt in a large bowl with the chopped-up lard and butter. You are aiming for a light, slightly flaky pastry.

Using a large palette knife, slowly add the water while cutting through the flour. When the pastry starts to come together, tip it out of the bowl on to a floured surface and work it lightly with your hands. You can still see small lumps of butter and lard.

Now get your rolling pin and lightly roll the pastry out to about 2cm thick. Fold one end over the other and roll again. Repeat the process twice more. By doing this you are trapping air within the pastry, which will give you the flaky finished product.

Wrap the pastry in clingfilm or greaseproof paper and leave it to rest in the fridge for at least half an hour.

Preheat the oven to 190°C. Chop the onion finely and put into a bowl with the meat. Peel the swede and potatoes, cut into small pieces, and put into a bowl of cold water (this helps to create steam within the sealed pasty, giving well-cooked, moist vegetables). When ready to put the pasties together, remove the swede and potatoes from the water and add to the onion and meat. Grate the butter into the mixture and season well with salt and freshly ground black pepper.

Take the pastry out of the fridge and divide into four. Roll each piece out into a circle, about the size of a tea plate. Brush the edge of the circle with beaten egg. Put a quarter of the filling down the middle of each of the circles, pressing the mixture firmly into place.

Now carefully bring the edges of the pastry up over the mixture and gently press together to seal the pasty. For a proper Cornish-pasty finish, you need to crimp the top. To do this, start at the corner of the pasty and put your forefinger on the back of the pastry, your thumb at the front. Cross your thumb over the top of your finger, effectively folding the pastry over. Now move your hand up the side and repeat the action. Continue until you reach the other side of the pasty and it is sealed.

Brush with egg and bake in the oven for half an hour. Reduce the temperature to 150°C and bake for a further 20 minutes.

To take with you for a picnic, wrap individually in baking parchment, then foil and a clean tea towel – this should keep them warm for a few hours.

FOR THE PASTRY

450g (1lb) plain flour

1 tablespoon of suet

Good pinch of salt

140g (5oz) lard, cold and cut into cubes

60g (2oz) butter, cold and cut into cubes

Cold water

FOR THE FILLING

110g (4oz) onion

340g (12oz) top of leg steak (rump or, traditionally, skirt) cut up into thin strips

220g (8oz) swede, peeled weight

220g (8oz) potato, peeled weight

60g (2oz) butter

Salt and black pepper

Cheese and ham quiche

SERVES 8

A classic quiche – rich, cheesy egg, with chunks of proper, home-cooked ham. If you haven't got any ham, just cut up some bacon into small pieces and fry it off in a dry frying pan.

Preheat the oven to 190°C. Roll out the pastry and use to line a large quiche dish (25cm in diameter). Line with tinfoil and fill with dried beans or a suitably sized cake tin to hold it down. Bake in the oven for 15 minutes. Remove foil and bake for a further 5 minutes. Reduce the oven temperature to 160°C.

In a small pan or microwave, soften the onion with the butter.

Put the softened onion into a bowl and add the eggs, cream, milk, cheese and ham with a really good grind of black pepper. Whisk together thoroughly. Carefully pour the mixture into the pastry case.

Bake in the bottom of the oven for about 35 minutes until golden brown, slightly risen and set in the middle. Allow to cool for at least 15 minutes before serving.

170g (6oz) shortcrust pastry (170g plain flour, 60g butter, 30g lard, water)

30g (1oz) butter

1 small onion, finely diced

8 eggs

300ml (½ pint) milk

150ml (¼ pint) double cream

170g (6oz) cooked ham

220g (8oz) mature Cheddar cheese

Ground black pepper

Broccoli and Blue Wensleydale quiche

SERVES 8

This is one of the most delicious quiches, with little nuggets of blue cheese when you bite into it. Blue Wensleydale is our local blue cheese and is ideal as it is creamy, subtle and melts well, but you could just as easily use a Blue Stilton, Yorkshire Blue or a blue cheese from your local area.

Preheat the oven to 190°C. Roll out the pastry and use to line a large quiche dish (30cm in diameter). Line with tinfoil and fill with dried beans or a suitably sized cake tin to hold it down. Bake in the oven for 15 minutes. Remove foil and bake for a further 5 minutes. Reduce the oven temperature to 160°C.

Bring a pan of water to the boil and add the florets of broccoli. Boil for 3 minutes then drain immediately and run cold water over the broccoli to stop it cooking any further.

Put the eggs, milk, cream, blue cheese, Cheddar and black pepper in a bowl and mix together well before adding the broccoli and stirring it in. Carefully pour the egg mixture into the pastry case.

Bake in the bottom of the oven for about 40 minutes until golden brown, slightly risen and set in the middle. Allow to cool for at least 15 minutes before serving.

170g (6oz) shortcrust pastry
(170g plain flour, 60g butter,
30g lard, water)

A good head of fresh broccoli

170g (6oz) Blue Wensleydale cheese,
cut into small cubes

170g (6oz) mature Cheddar cheese,
grated

8 eggs

300ml (½ pint) milk

150ml (¼ pint) cream

Ground black pepper

Asparagus quiche

In the North of England, at around the beginning of May, the new-season asparagus starts to appear in the shops. The deep green colour, crisp texture and unique taste are delicious indicators of the start of summer. Simply served with butter and brown bread is enough for a quick lunch, or whizzed into a velvety soup is another favourite. This is a quick and easy quiche which, combined with a tasty salad and some new potatoes, makes a perfect early-summer lunch.

Preheat the oven to 190°C. Roll out the pastry and use to line a large quiche dish (25cm in diameter). Line with tinfoil and fill with dried beans or a suitably sized cake tin to hold it down. Bake in the oven for 15 minutes. Remove foil and bake for a further 5 minutes. Reduce the oven temperature to 160°C.

Break the ends off the asparagus and discard. Cut the rest of the asparagus into 2cm pieces, leaving the tops of the spears whole. Bring a pan of salted water to the boil and add the asparagus. Boil for 3 minutes then drain immediately and run cold water over the asparagus to stop it cooking any further.

Pick out the spears and keep to one side to decorate the top of the quiche.

Put the pieces of asparagus, eggs, milk, cream, cheese and black pepper in a bowl and mix together well. Carefully pour the mixture into the pastry case. Arrange the spears on top like the hands on a clock.

Bake in the bottom of the oven for about 40 minutes until golden brown, slightly risen and set in the middle.

170g (6oz) shortcrust pastry (170g plain flour, 60g butter, 30g lard, water)

A bunch of fresh English asparagus

8 eggs

300ml (½ pint) milk

150ml (¼ pint) cream

220g (8oz) mature Cheddar cheese

Ground black pepper

Doreen's cherry tomato and Wensleydale cheese tartlets

SERVES 6

Doreen served these delicious little tartlets to her guests at Butt House. She has used a vegetarian lard, Trex, to keep the pastry suitable for vegetarians. Serve warm with dressed salad leaves

To make the pastry, sieve the flour, ground rice and salt into a large bowl and rub in the Trex until it resembles breadcrumbs. Using a knife, mix in the beaten egg and then add the water one spoonful at a time, until the pastry comes together into a ball. On a floured surface, roll the pastry out thinly and cut into six rounds using a small saucer.

Grease well six 9cm-diameter loose-bottomed small flan cases, and line with the pastry.

Cut the tomatoes in half, and place four halves in each case. Sprinkle the cheese round and on top of the tomatoes. Mix the eggs and milk together and pour over the tomatoes and cheese, taking care not to overfill.

Place on a baking sheet and bake at 180°C for around 30 minutes until set and lightly browned.

FOR THE PASTRY

310g (11oz) self-raising flour

30g (1oz) ground rice

A pinch of salt

140g (5oz) Trex

1 beaten egg

Cold water

FOR THE FILLING

12 cherry tomatoes

85g (3oz) Wensleydale cheese, grated

2 eggs, beaten

210ml (7fl oz) milk

Quick teatime risotto

This is a great way to use up leftovers the day after having roast chicken for supper. If you are short on fresh vegetables, add some frozen peas or broad beans 5 minutes before the end of cooking, to boost the nutritional content. You can also stir in cooked sausages or bacon from breakfast or some ham, if required.

In a pan over a medium heat, gently fry the onion in the olive oil until soft and then add the garlic, taking care not to brown.

Add the rice and other vegetables and continue to cook for a good 6 to 7 minutes until the vegetables are softening.

Start to add the stock, a little at a time, allowing the liquid to be absorbed before adding any more (it probably won't take all the stock). Season with salt and a good grind of black pepper. Reduce the heat to minimum and simmer the risotto until the rice is soft and the consistency is that of creamy rice pudding.

At this stage, if you have any leftover roast chicken or pieces of cooked sausage or bacon, add it to the risotto and allow to warm through properly.

Just before serving, stir in the cheese and allow to melt. Serve immediately with salad.

1 small onion, finely chopped

Olive oil

2 cloves of garlic, finely chopped

220g (8oz) arborio risotto rice

1 red or yellow pepper, deseeded and sliced

1 courgette, chopped

1 chicken stock cube, dissolved in 450ml (¾ pint) of boiling water

Salt and black pepper

110g (4oz) mature Cheddar cheese

The environs of Deer 'n Dexter's farm at Stoddah, Penrith

Lemon, thyme and pinenut risotto

This is the perfect way to eat a roast chicken or lightly poached salmon on a summer's evening – hopefully sitting with friends in the garden with some chilled white wine. Ideally, roast the chicken just before making the risotto, so that you can use all the buttery juices out of the pan to soften the onion.

In a pan over a medium heat, soften the onion and garlic in either the juices from the chicken roasting pan or in the butter and olive oil. When softened, add the rice and allow to cook for a few minutes, stirring occasionally.

Add the wine, lemon juice and rind and allow to absorb into the rice, stirring occasionally. When the wine is absorbed, slowly add the stock (or boiling water, if you are using the chicken juices), letting the liquid absorb before you add any more. Season with salt, if needed, and a good grind of black pepper.

Reduce the heat to minimum and simmer until the rice is softened and the consistency is that of creamy rice pudding. Add the Cheddar cheese, thyme and pinenuts.

Put into a large bowl and top with rocket and thick shavings of Parmesan (use a potato peeler). Serve with warm chicken or salmon.

If you are serving vegetarians, use the risotto to stuff large yellow peppers – simply cut round the stalk of the pepper, carefully remove the seeds and fibre from the inside, stuff with the risotto and put into an ovenproof dish lined with cherry tomatoes. Cover with foil and bake in the oven at 170°C for about 40 minutes until the pepper is soft. Serve with the rocket and Parmesan on the side.

1 medium onion, finely chopped

2 cloves of garlic, finely chopped

1 dessertspoon of olive oil

30g (1oz) butter

220g (8oz) arborio risotto rice

150ml (¼ pint) white wine

Rind and juice of a lemon

Salt and black pepper

1 chicken stock cube, dissolved in 300ml (½ pint) of boiling water

1 tablespoon of fresh thyme, finely chopped

110g (4oz) mature Cheddar cheese, grated

60g (2oz) pinenuts

60g (2oz) Parmesan cheese

1 bag of rocket leaves, washed

Macaroni cheese with bacon

Comfort food at its best! Creamy macaroni ideally served with baked tomatoes on the vine and bacon – simple, full of flavour and easy to prepare in advance.

Preheat the oven to 180°C. Cook the pasta as instructed on the packet.

In a pan over a medium heat, melt the butter and stir in the flour. Off the heat, gradually whisk in the milk until smooth. Add the mustard and a good grind of black pepper and return to the heat. Cook until the sauce is thickened and boiling, stirring frequently to avoid it sticking to the bottom of the pan.

Remove from the heat and stir in the cheese. Pour the pasta into the sauce and mix well. Put the macaroni cheese in an ovenproof dish. Chop the bacon into thin strips over the top of the macaroni and arrange the tomatoes around the edge.

Bake in the oven for about 20 minutes until the bacon is golden brown and the tomatoes are cooked. Serve immediately.

220g (8oz) macaroni pasta

60g (2oz) butter

60g (2oz) flour

600ml (1 pint) milk

Half a teaspoon of English mustard

Black pepper

220g (8oz) mature Cheddar cheese

4 ripe tomatoes, halved, or 8 cherry tomatoes

8 rashers of bacon

Pizza

Pizza is a quick, easy and versatile way of feeding a large group of people. You can either use a bread base or, if you haven't got time for the bread-making process, use 450g of cheese scone mixture (see page 80) instead. The tomato sauce is a staple which is handy to have as an instant pasta sauce – it will keep in the fridge for up to a week. Wrapped in parchment paper and then tinfoil, pizzas travel well and make a substantial midday meal for a lengthy walk.

In a large bowl, mix the flour, salt and yeast together. Make a well in the middle and add the olive oil. Slowly add the warm water, stirring all the time. When the mixture starts to form a dough, turn it out on to a floured surface. Knead the dough with your hands for about 5 minutes, until it becomes smooth and pliant. Put back into the bowl, cover with a tea towel and leave in a warm place for about an hour.

While the dough is rising, you can make the tomato sauce. In a pan, soften the onion in the oil. Add the garlic and stir for a further minute. Add the tomatoes, purée and herbs with the salt and pepper. Bring to the boil, then reduce the heat. Simmer for a good 20 minutes until the sauce thickens and becomes darker.

When the dough has doubled in size, turn it on to a floured surface and knead it for a minute. At this stage, you can put the dough in a fridge or freezer to use later. If using straight away, roll the dough into the required shape and assemble the pizza.

Preheat the oven to 200°C. Put enough tomato sauce on to the dough to cover the surface. You don't want too much sauce as the toppings will slide off when you cut the pizza.

Top with whatever you like – salami, peppers, mushrooms, olives, proscuitto, little sprigs of thyme, oregano. Put in the oven for 15 minutes, then top with cheese – mature Cheddar, feta, mozzarella – and return to the oven for a further 10 minutes until the dough is golden brown.

Cut into pieces and serve immediately with a dressed green salad.

FOR A BREAD BASE

750g (1½lb) strong white bread flour (or a mix of white and wholemeal)

1 teaspoon of salt

1 packet of easy-blend yeast

2 tablespoons of olive oil

Warm water to mix

FOR TOMATO SAUCE

1 medium onion, finely diced

1 tablespoon of olive oil

2 cloves of garlic, finely chopped

1 x 400g (14oz) tin of peeled plum, chopped or cherry tomatoes

1 tablespoon of tomato purée

1 tablespoon of chopped mixed fresh herbs, such as thyme, oregano, rosemary

A pinch of salt and a good grind of black pepper

Scotch eggs

These are nothing like the bright-orange-coloured, hard Scotch eggs you can buy. They are crunchy on the outside with a creamy free-range egg in the middle like a little parcel. You can vary the flavour by varying the sausage meat – for children perhaps use ordinary pork sausage meat, for adults maybe a stronger-flavoured Cumberland sausage meat with more herbs and texture. They are easy to make but do be careful with the hot fat (which you will need to strain through kitchen paper when it is cool due to the breadcrumbs). If taking on a picnic, make sure you cool them down properly before packing them up, as they will sweat and go soggy if put in a bag while warm.

4 free-range eggs

450g (1lb) sausage meat

1 egg, beaten

2 slices of bread, made into crumbs

In a pan, bring the eggs to the boil and then continue to boil for a further 6 minutes. Run the pan under cold water for a couple of minutes until totally cold. Peel the eggs and dry them on clean kitchen roll.

Divide the sausage meat into four and, taking one piece, roll it between your palms to form a ball and then flatten it. Take the egg and put it into the middle of the meat. Mould the sausage meat carefully round it until there are no gaps and the egg is evenly covered.

Roll the covered egg in the beaten egg and then in the breadcrumbs. Repeat the process for the other three eggs.

Either in a large pan, or a deep fat fryer if you have one, bring the heat up to medium and lower the eggs into the hot fat, using a slotted spoon. Keep turning the eggs as they brown in the fat for about 12 minutes. Remove from the fat with the slotted spoon on to a plate lined with kitchen roll.

Either serve immediately or allow to cool without covering.

Wensleydale mushrooms   SERVES 4 AS A STARTER OR 2 FOR LUNCH

Wensleydale is a crumbly cheese which doesn't melt well, making it ideal for this dish as it leaves little nuggets in a rich sauce. Elizabeth's sister Susie invented this recipe when feeling really peckish and using up what was in the fridge. It makes a tasty lunch on thick-cut granary toast or an equally good starter, served in ramekins.

In a pan, soften the mushrooms and bacon in the butter. When cooked, add the flour and stir in well. Keep stirring for a further minute to cook the flour.

Remove from the heat and slowly whisk in the milk and pepper (you won't need salt due to the smoked bacon and cheese). Put back on to hob and stir continuously until boiling. Remove from the heat and add the Cheddar cheese.

Cut the Wensleydale cheese into little cubes and add to the mushroom mixture.

If serving lunch for two, simply spread on toasted granary bread, or, for a starter, divide into four ramekins, sprinkle with a little Cheddar cheese and place under a hot grill until golden brown and bubbling.

170g (6oz) mushrooms, sliced

4 rashers of smoked bacon

60g (2oz) butter

30g (1oz) plain flour

210ml (⅓ pint) whole milk

Black pepper

110g (4oz) Wensleydale cheese

110g (4oz) mature Cheddar cheese, grated

Barns, walls and flower meadows in Wensleydale

Granny Baker's bean soup

Elizabeth's mother lived in Valencia, Spain for a year, where she became a regular at the spectacular indoor food market, one of the best in the world and a culinary feast for both the eye and the palate. This is one of her recipes from that time: hearty, chunky and flavoursome.

In a large casserole dish, soften the onions with the olive oil. Add the garlic, peppers and sweet potatoes and continue to stir for about 5 minutes until starting to soften. Add the rest of the ingredients except the parsley.

Bring to the boil and then simmer for an hour. Sprinkle with chopped parsley just before serving.

2 medium onions, finely chopped

A tablespoon of olive oil

2 cloves of garlic, finely chopped

2 red peppers and 1 green pepper, deseeded and chopped

2 sweet potatoes, chopped and diced into 1cm pieces

450g (1lb) cannellini beans, soaked overnight and then boiled and simmered for 1¼ hours, or 2 x 400g (14oz) tins of mixed beans

1x 400g (14oz) tin of chopped tomatoes

1 carton or jar of passata

170g (6oz) chorizo sausage, cut into small chunks

600ml (1 pint) of chicken stock or 1 vegetarian stock cube, dissolved in 600ml (1 pint) of boiling water

1 tablespoon of Spanish pimenton or smoked paprika

A handful of freshly chopped, flat-leaf parsley

Vegetable soup

What is better than a good vegetable soup when you need a little comforting on a chilly day in the middle of a long walk? The base of this soup is always the same – onion, potatoes and stock – and, from there, you can add whatever vegetables you have to hand. For a traditional vegetable soup, we have used carrots, swede and parsnips, but leeks, celery, celeriac and many others will make a tasty change.

In a large pan over a medium heat, melt the butter and soften the onion but do not brown. Peel the vegetables and cut them into evenly sized pieces. Add the vegetables to the onion and stir for about 5 minutes until they are starting to soften and lightly brown.

Add the stock with a little salt and a good grind of black pepper. Bring to the boil, then put the lid on the pan, reduce the temperature to minimum and simmer for about 20 minutes until the vegetables are soft.

Use a blender to give a rich, smooth texture, adding a little water if the texture is too thick.

Serve immediately with chunks of fresh bread and butter.

1 medium onion, finely diced

60g (2oz) butter

3 medium potatoes

3 carrots

3 parsnips

Half a swede

900ml (1½ pints) fresh chicken stock and 1 chicken stock cube or 2 vegetable stock cubes, dissolved in 900ml (1½ pints) of boiling water

Salt and black pepper

Parsnip and celeriac soup

SERVES 4

This is a delicious, rich soup which tastes smooth and creamy even without adding any cream. The celeriac stops it from being too sweet and, once tried, you will make it time and time again. Stirring a teaspoon of cumin powder into the onion gives a lightly spiced alternative.

Peel and chop all the vegetables into similar sized, small pieces. Melt the butter in a pan and add the onion. Allow to soften for a couple of minutes and then stir in the rest of the vegetables. Continue to stir for about 5 minutes until the vegetables are starting to brown in the butter.

2 large potatoes

Half a celeriac

2 large parsnips

60g (2oz) butter

1 medium onion, finely diced

Add the stock with a pinch of salt and a good grind of black pepper. Bring to the boil, cover and simmer for about 15 minutes until all the vegetables are soft. Blend until smooth and serve with a swirl of cream. For a lower-fat version, soften the onion in a teaspoon of olive oil, add the vegetables and stock without stirring in the butter and omit cream when serving.

1 chicken stock cube, dissolved in 600ml (1 pint) of boiling water

Salt and black pepper

2 tablespoons of cream

Mushroom soup

SERVES 4

This recipe is a smooth, pureed soup but, for a special alternative, you can add some butter-fried mushrooms with garlic and parsley just before serving. If you can find field mushrooms, they give the best flavour, colour and texture, but for the most part you will just have to use ordinary mushrooms. It is delicious served with chunky slices of granary bread.

In a large pan, melt the butter and soften the onion. Add the potatoes and mushrooms and stir for 5 minutes while they get coated in the butter and start to soften.

1 medium onion, finely diced

60g (2oz) butter

2 large potatoes, peeled and diced

Add the stock and milk and season well with a good pinch of salt and plenty of black pepper. Bring to the boil and then reduce the heat to minimum and simmer for about 15 minutes until the vegetables are soft.

220g (8oz) mushrooms

1 vegetable stock cube, dissolved in 300ml (½ pint) of boiling water

300ml (½ pint) milk

Blend the soup until smooth and adjust the seasoning if necessary.

Salt and black pepper

Doreen's tomato soup

SERVES 4

This is one of Doreen's signature soups and one which her returning guests always requested.

Melt the butter in a saucepan, add the onion and tomatoes, and fry until soft.

Add the stock and tin of tomatoes and simmer until cooked. Liquidise or blend with a hand blender, then sieve to remove the seeds and skin, and return to the saucepan. Add the tomato purée and sugar.

Season to taste, bring to the boil, and serve with a garnish of finely chopped basil.

60g (2oz) butter

1 medium onion, finely diced

2 large, ripe tomatoes, chopped

1 vegetable stock cube, dissolved in 450ml (¾ pint) of boiling water

1x 400g (14oz) tin of chopped tomatoes

2 teaspoons of tomato purée

2 teaspoons of sugar

Salt and pepper

Carrot and coriander soup

SERVES 4

In Elizabeth's house, this is definitely Granny's soup and the children love it. It is gently flavoursome and aromatic and, with its rich orange colour, it makes an inviting dish, whatever the season.

In a pan, soften the onion in the butter, then add the carrots, potato and ground coriander and stir for a couple of minutes.

Add the stock, a pinch of salt and a good grind of black pepper. Cover the pan, reduce the heat to minimum and simmer for 25 minutes until the vegetables are tender.

Blend the soup until smooth and stir in the chopped fresh coriander. Serve with crusty baguettes.

1 medium onion, finely diced

60g (2oz) butter

4 large carrots, peeled and chopped

1 potato, peeled and chopped

2 teaspoons of ground coriander

1 chicken stock cube, dissolved in 750ml (1¼ pints) of boiling water

Salt and black pepper

A good handful of fresh coriander, chopped

Watercress soup

This is an all-time favourite summer soup – it is peppery and fresh with a lovely bright green colour and it is so packed with goodness you feel healthier just eating it! If you can get a bunch of fresh watercress from your greengrocer it is ideal or alternatively you can buy a bag from most supermarkets, although nutritionally this will not be as good as the fresh leaves.

In a large pan over a medium heat, melt the butter and soften the onion but do not brown. Peel the potatoes and cut them into small cubes. Add the potatoes to the pan and stir to coat in the butter but, again, do not brown.

Pour in the chicken or vegetable stock with a little salt and a good grind of black pepper. Bring to the boil and then put the lid on the pan and simmer for about 15 minutes until the potatoes are soft.

To prepare the watercress, cut off the very ends but leave the stalks (if you have a bag, it will have been prepared) and wash it thoroughly in a colander. Add to the soup when it is cooked with the cream and blend until you have a really smooth, creamy consistency.

Check the seasoning and serve with a small swirl of double cream and a sprig of watercress in each bowl. Perfect with thick-cut, generously buttered granary bread.

1 medium onion, finely diced

60g (2oz) butter

3 medium potatoes

900ml (1½ pints) fresh chicken stock and 1 chicken stock cube or 2 vegetable stock cubes, dissolved in 900ml (1½ pints) of boiling water

Salt and black pepper

150ml (¼ pint) double cream

1 bunch or bag of fresh watercress, washed

Homemade beefburgers

We have made hearty, quarter-pounders here, which are quite filling but there is nothing to stop you making them to suit your own needs. If you are having a barbecue with a variety of foods on offer, simply make little burgers to feed greater numbers. You can make these in batches and freeze them as they can be cooked from frozen and are handy for unexpected guests. If you are feeling adventurous, you could pack a camping stove for a hike, and cook them whilst admiring a fantastic view. They work just as well using minced lamb and chopped mint instead of beef and parsley.

Mix all the ingredients together in a large bowl.

Wet your hands to stop the mince sticking to them. Take approximately 110g (4oz) of mince (a palmful), and shape into a ball. Flatten your palms together to give a burger shape about 1½cm thick.

Either fry or barbecue, for about 5 minutes on each side, until brown and cooked through. Serve in large fresh bread buns with butter-fried onions and sliced beef tomatoes.

If not using immediately, put the uncooked burgers on to a baking tray lined with parchment paper. Cover with more parchment and put into the fridge or freezer until you need them. When frozen, remove the burgers from the tray and put them into a plastic bag in the freezer.

1kg (2.2lb) lean minced beef

1 medium onion, finely diced

1 free-range egg

A good handful of finely chopped fresh herbs, such as parsley, thyme, oregano, rosemary

Salt and black pepper

Chicken liver and orange pâté

SERVES 6

Chicken livers are inexpensive and quick to cook. They are delicious sliced up with smoked bacon and fried in butter for a salad topping or cut up into terrines. This pâté has a mild fragrance of orange that gives a simple but flavoursome result.

Firstly, prepare the chicken livers. Take each liver and cut it in half. If it has a small, greenish-looking sac attached, you must remove and discard it – it is very bitter which will spoil the finished dish.

In a pan, melt the butter and soften the onion without browning. Add the garlic and continue to cook for a further minute. Remove from the pan, leaving the butter. Add the livers to the pan and brown on all sides. Reduce the heat and continue to cook for 5 minutes.

Put the livers and onion, with the orange zest, into a food processor or liquidiser and pulse until really smooth. At this stage, you can add the cream, if you want a really creamy texture.

Spoon the pâté into a large pot or separate ramekins. Allow to cool and then put in the fridge to set.

The pâté will keep for three to four days. For a special party, it is attractive to put a thin layer of clarified butter over the top of the pâté, once it has set. This will seal it and it will keep safely in the fridge for up to a week.

1 x 450g (1lb) pack of chicken livers

1 medium onion, finely diced

110g (4oz) butter

2 cloves of garlic, peeled and crushed

Zest of an orange

2 tablespoons of double cream (optional)

Blue Wensleydale and walnut pâté

This pâté is easy to make and is a delicious combination, with the tang of the blue cheese and the crunch of walnuts. It can be used as a stuffing for chicken breasts (see page 122), when it melts and makes its own irresistible sauce, or as a pâté in a baguette with slices of Cox's apples. It is also a really good alternative cheese on toast, just grilled on toasted bread. We use our local Blue Wensleydale but you can of course use your own local hard blue, such as Stilton or Buxton Blue.

In a bowl, mash the two cheeses together thoroughly and stir in the walnuts.

It will keep in the fridge in a sealed container for four to five days. Use as required.

170g (6oz) Blue Wensleydale cheese

110g (4oz) full-fat soft cream cheese

110g (4oz) walnuts, chopped

Doreen's hummus

Although not a pâté as such, hummus is convenient to serve with pitta bread as a quick lunch or starter.

Place all the ingredients in a liquidiser and liquidise until smooth.

Put in ramekin dishes and leave to stand, for at least an hour, for the flavours to blend. Serve with crudités or toast.

1 x 400g (14oz) can of chick peas, drained

2 cloves of garlic, finely chopped or crushed

2 tablespoons of tahini paste

4 tablespoons of olive oil

2 tablespoons of lemon juice

Salt and pepper

Smoked trout pâté

SERVES 4

Fresh smoked trout is such a treat. It is delicious flaked into a quiche or on to softly scrambled egg, but it also makes a perfect pâté. The smokiness of the fish, combined with the tang of the horseradish and lemon, makes the addition of any salt unnecessary. Simply serve with thinly sliced brown bread.

Combine all the ingredients in a food processor and blend until smooth.

Divide between four small ramekins and decorate with a slice of lemon and flat-leaf parsley.

If you don't have a food processor, mash all the ingredients together with a fork until you have an even consistency.

This recipe works just as well with smoked salmon.

170g (6oz) smoked trout

110g (4oz) crème fraîche or soft cream cheese

2 teaspoons of horseradish sauce

Juice of ½ lemon

A good grind of black pepper

SWALEDALE CHEESE

You would never look in either of our fridges without finding cheese of some description. Always a good mature Cheddar for a quick snack and a variety of other cheeses, depending on where we have visited. Particularly with a family, if you have eggs, milk and cheese in the house, you are never far away from a quick, satisfying meal.

As with many areas of food production, the return to traditionally crafted cheesemaking has had a marked effect on attitudes to the cheese industry and on consumer interest in the sector. In the second half of the twentieth century British cheese had a miserable reputation for poor quality and taste, with a few famous exceptions. With the advent of farmers' markets, however, it has undergone a transformation and now has superb cheeses to enhance any cheeseboard. In any area of the UK, you would not have to venture far to find a cheesemaker using local milk to make excellent cheeses. Around the Coast to Coast route alone, there are many highly respected cheeses – Mrs Kirkham's Lancashire, Hawes Wensleydale, Yorkshire Blue and Cotherstone to name but a few favourites.

Walking through Lower Swaledale in summer, you can't fail to notice the distinctive black and white cows of the dairy herds, grazing on the rich meadows flanking the River Swale. In days gone by, making cheese was a way of preserving the milk and was a skill employed by most farmers' wives. Many farms would have a sign on the gate, selling eggs, milk and cheese to supplement their income. Over the years, as farmers' wives have gone out to work and people have become more mobile, the country cheesemaker was disappearing. By the mid 1980s, local farmer Mrs Longstaff was the last person from whom you could buy farmhouse Swaledale cheese.

One of the few commercial outlets for Mrs Longstaff's cheese was the well-known and respected Black Bull at Moulton. When she sold her smallholding in 1987, it looked as if Swaledale cheese production was finished. However, David Reed, the chef at the Black Bull, with his wife Mandy, made the life-changing decision to secure the future of Swaledale cheese by taking over the recipe from Mrs Longstaff and setting up the Swaledale Cheese Company.

In the early days, David and Mandy made the cheese in their kitchen. Soon it became clear that combining a young family with hygienic production was becoming impossible and they converted some outbuildings to a dairy. When they again outgrew the facilities and were refused planning permission to extend on their own site, they had to move to commercial premises in Richmond. Such a development, however, did not compromise the quality of the cheese, with David ensuring that all milk still came from farms along the Swale.

Each of the 14 varieties is made by hand using traditional methods and slowly matured for maximum flavour. The original cow's and ewe's milk Swaledales are the first Yorkshire cheeses to have Protected Designation of Origin status from the EU and have enjoyed huge success at national and international shows.

Sadly David died suddenly in 2005 but the company is still run by Mandy and their two grown-up children, Louise and Sam. Despite their success, the Reeds are determined to keep the company small, believing that quality and personal service always come first. Each part of the process, from sourcing the milk from local farms to hand waxing the individual cheeses, is done with the utmost care and attention. For the Reed family, cheese is not just their livelihood, but their life.

SWEET TREATS

Every good walker needs a 'pick-me-up' en route and a proper picnic is not the same without some cake. Ideally, you need something fairly solid that will withstand the rigours of the day, high in energy and yet a sweet treat at the same time.

Good packing and sensible food go a long way to making a packed lunch all the more enjoyable. Try to plan what will travel well and put it all in separate containers – it makes the end result so much more inviting.

Baking is arguably the most enjoyable part of cookery – it fills the kitchen with inviting aromas, is always greeted with enthusiasm and is almost always delicious. We prefer to make all our cakes and tray bakes – they may not last as long as some of the manufactured offerings but at least you know they have no preservatives or stabilisers added. We're always suspicious of a flapjack or brownie that can keep 'fresh' for six months or more. Once you become confident at home baking and get to know the little quirks of your oven, you will hopefully find it quite therapeutic and start to try different recipes.

Doreen's renowned chocolate cake

This is the recipe for the chocolate cake which Doreen and Ernest gave to their guests on arrival; it also happens to be a favourite of their local MP.

Preheat the oven to 150°C. Beat together the margarine and sugar until light and fluffy. Add the eggs a couple at a time and beat in, then add the cocoa to the flour and sieve into mixture. Finally, add the water and mix well before spooning the mixture into two well-greased 18cm cake tins, lined with parchment paper.

Bake for about 30 minutes until risen and lightly firm to the touch.

Put the icing sugar, cocoa powder and margarine in a bowl and mix together. If needed, add a little milk to soften the mixture.

When the cake is cool, turn the bottom cake over so that it is upside down on the plate on which you are going to serve it. Put half of the icing on to the cake and place the other cake on top, baked side up. Cover with the rest of the icing and make criss-cross marks with a fork.

FOR THE CAKE

220g (8oz) margarine

220g (8oz) caster sugar

4 eggs

220g (8oz) self-raising flour

2 teaspoons of cocoa powder

2–3 tablespoons of warm water

FOR THE ICING

220g (8oz) sifted icing sugar

110g (4oz) margarine

1 tablespoon of cocoa powder

A small amount of milk, if needed

Coffee cake

A lovely moist sponge cake, enhanced by the crunch of walnuts. You can either use liquid Camp coffee or fairly strong instant coffee mixed with a small amount of hot water. You will need two 25cm cake tins, lightly buttered and lined with parchment paper.

Preheat the oven to 150°C. Put the margarine and caster sugar in a bowl and mix until pale and fluffy. Break the eggs into a small bowl, add to the butter mixture and gently mix. Add the coffee. With a spatula, bring all the mixture down from the side of the bowl and add the flour. Mix well but do not overbeat. Divide the mixture into two tins and spread out evenly.

Place in the middle of the oven for about 30 minutes, until risen in the middle and softly firm to the touch. With a knife, carefully ease the cake from the side of the tin. Turn out on to a cooling rack.

Put the icing sugar and margarine in a bowl and mix together. Add the coffee and then the milk, a little at a time, and whisk until smooth and soft.

When the cake is cool, turn the bottom cake over so that it is upside down on the plate on which you are going to serve it. Put half of the icing on to the cake and place the other cake on top, baked side up. Cover with the rest of the icing and use a good handful of walnuts to decorate.

FOR THE CAKE

280g (10oz) margarine

280g (10oz) caster sugar

5 eggs

2 tablespoons of Camp coffee

280g (10oz) self-raising flour

FOR THE ICING

280g (10oz) sifted icing sugar

140g (5oz) margarine

1 tablespoon of Camp coffee

A small amount of milk

A handful of chopped walnuts

Classic Victoria sponge

A really good light sponge deserves a really good homemade or artisan jam – preferably raspberry or strawberry. Bake it as a traditional round double cake using two cake tins.

Make this cake in the same way as the coffee cake on page 62, omitting the coffee. Replace the icing with jam in the middle and a sprinkle of caster sugar on top. If you like you can put butter icing in the middle with the jam – make it by mixing 110g (4oz) icing sugar with 60g (2oz) of butter and a small amount of milk to soften.

To make buns for children, use a 110g (4oz) mixture of plain sponge, which will give you 10 large buns. Use muffin cases and a deep Yorkshire pudding tin to give a nice big bun. Decorate with icing sugar (about 220g) softened with a little cold water and coloured with an edible food colouring of your choice. You can make butterflies and caterpillars out of white chocolate buttons with hundreds and thousands or you can get really pretty sprinkles that look like glitter, and jelly sweets or Smarties never fail to earn a smile.

Lemon drizzle cake

This is a light-as-air sponge with a tangy layer of lemony sugar on the top – everyone's favourite on the tea table. The ingredients and method are the same as for the lemon curd cake on page 67, but you will need two lemons, juice and zest, not one. Instead of icing and lemon curd, you need a sugar syrup made from the juice of the two lemons, 110g (4oz) caster sugar and 110g (4oz) granulated sugar. The mixture is enough to make two loaf-shaped cakes (freeze one for later use) or one tray bake.

FOR LOAVES

Grease two 1lb loaf tins and line with parchment paper. Divide the mixture between the two tins and bake in the centre of the oven, preheated to 150°C, for about 30 minutes until the loaves are well risen, golden brown and softly firm to the touch.

FOR A TRAY BAKE

Grease a 30cm x 20cm baking tray and line with parchment paper. Put the mixture into the tin and spread out evenly. Bake in the centre of the oven, preheated to 150°C, for about 30 minutes until well risen, golden brown and softly firm to the touch.

Whilst the cakes are in the oven, put the lemon juice in a bowl with the granulated and caster sugars and stir until you have a thick syrup. As soon as the cake comes out of the oven, carefully spoon the lemon syrup over the cake, making sure you cover the top. Allow to cool completely in the tins.

Lemon curd cake

Make lemon curd at the same time as meringues so as not to waste the egg yolks. It is so tangy and delicious (especially on hot, buttered toast) and has no preservatives as in many manufactured curds. Lemon curd must be kept in the fridge.

Put all the ingredients in a pan and melt over a low heat, stirring continuously. Bring to the boil and simmer for about 3 to 5 minutes until the curd is glossy.

Put into a clean jar or bowl and cool.

Put the icing sugar into a bowl and slowly add the lemon juice until you have a soft but not runny icing.

You will need two 25cm cake tins, lightly buttered and lined with parchment paper.

Preheat the oven to 150°C. Put the margarine and caster sugar in a bowl and mix until pale and fluffy. Break the eggs into a small bowl, add to the butter mixture and gently mix. With a spatula, bring all the mixture down from the side of the bowl and add the flour and lemon zest. Mix well but do not overbeat. Divide the mixture into two tins and spread out evenly.

Place in the middle of the oven for about 30 minutes, until risen in the middle and softly firm to the touch. With a knife, carefully ease the cake from the side of the tin. Turn out on to a cooling rack.

When the cake is cool, turn the bottom one over so that it is upside down on the plate on which you are going to serve it. Put on enough lemon curd to cover the cake and place the other cake on top, baked side up. Cover the top with the lemon icing.

This is a beautiful cake, particularly for Easter, when you can decorate with crystallised primroses and violets – just dip the flowers in beaten egg white, then into caster sugar and allow to dry completely on parchment paper. Arrange in the middle of the cake.

FOR THE CURD

Zest and juice of a large lemon

110g (4oz) granulated sugar

2 egg yolks or 1 large free-range egg

60g (2oz) butter

FOR THE ICING

110g (4oz) icing sugar

Lemon juice (about a dessertspoon)

FOR THE CAKE

280g (10oz) margarine

280g (10oz) caster sugar

5 eggs

280g (10oz) self-raising flour

Zest of a large lemon

Carrot cake with mascarpone and orange icing   SERVES 12

This is a wonderful combination of soft, moist cake and cool, fresh creamy topping – it is so easy to make and always feels a little healthier than traditional cakes. It is a good recipe to make with children and can be put into individual muffin tins.

Preheat the oven to 150°C. Grease a 30cm x 20cm baking tin and line with parchment paper. In a large bowl, add all the ingredients for the cake and mix together thoroughly.

Pour the mixture into the tin and place in the centre of the oven for about 35 minutes, until the cake is well risen, golden brown and lightly firm to the touch. Lift on to a rack and allow to cool completely.

To make the icing, put all the ingredients in a bowl and mix together. Spread over the top of the cake and cut into 12 squares.

FOR THE CAKE

340g (12oz) carrots (peeled and grated)

4 eggs

220g (8oz) soft brown sugar

180ml (6fl oz) vegetable oil

220g (8oz) self-raising flour (can be wholemeal)

110g (4oz) coconut

110g (4oz) raisins

1 teaspoon of mixed spice and ½ teaspoon of freshly grated nutmeg

FOR THE TOPPING

1 tub of mascarpone cheese (if you can't get mascarpone, use full-fat soft cheese)

1 tablespoon of icing sugar

Zest of an orange

Date and walnut loaf

SERVES 8–10

Anything involving dates gets a refusal from most children as they think they don't like them. However, sticky toffee pudding and this recipe are always popular – dates in disguise! This is a lovely sticky loaf which is delicious on its own or buttered – ideal for a packed lunch or picnic. It keeps well and freezes, so it's worth doubling the recipe and making two at the same time.

Preheat the oven to 150°C. Grease a 1kg (2lb) loaf tin and line with parchment paper.

In a bowl, pour the boiling water over the dates and bicarbonate of soda. As it cools, the dates will soften.

In a separate bowl or food mixer, cream the sugar and butter together until pale and then add the egg. Stir in the flour, nuts and finally the date mixture.

Put the mixture in the tin and bake in the centre of the oven for about 1¼ hours until well risen, golden brown and firm to the touch. Allow to cool completely before serving.

To keep, wrap firmly in clingfilm or foil and it will stay fresh for at least two weeks.

220g (8oz) finely chopped dates

Half a teaspoon of bicarbonate of soda

150ml (¼ pint) boiling water

85g (3oz) butter

85g (3oz) soft brown sugar

1 egg

220g (8oz) self-raising flour

85g (3oz) walnuts

Buttermere and Fleetwith Pike

Local ale fruit loaf

As this loaf can be stored for up to six weeks, it's a good idea to make two at a time. It has no added fat except for the eggs, so can be suitable for those on a low-fat diet (if you don't serve it with cheese, that is!). We have used Wold Top Brewery ale (see page 93) for this recipe, but you could use any good bottled ale from a brewery in your area.

Put the dried fruit and sugar into a large pan and cover with the bottled beer. Gently heat the fruit until the beer is hot. Remove from the heat, cover and leave overnight.

Preheat the oven to 140°C. Add the flours, mixed spice and eggs to the fruit mixture. Stir well until all the ingredients are combined. Divide the mixture between two greased loaf tins, lined with parchment paper.

Bake in the oven for 1¼ hours until risen, pale brown and firm to the touch.

Cover with a tea towel and leave in the tins to cool. Wrap tightly in clingfilm and store in a cool, dry place.

Delicious on its own or buttered or served with a piece of Hawes Wensleydale cheese.

450g (1lb) small currants

140g (5oz) raisins

140g (5oz) peel

1 x 500ml bottle of strong beer such as Wold Top Brewery ale

170g (6oz) soft dark brown sugar

170g (6oz) white self-raising flour

170g (6oz) wholemeal self-raising flour

3 teaspoons of mixed spice

3 eggs

Doreen's fruit cake

SERVES AT LEAST 20

It is so good to have a fruit-cake recipe you can trust – this is the one. Doreen has kept it close to her chest for over 25 years, despite numerous requests. We're very honoured! As with all fruit-based cakes, it keeps very well, making it ideal for taking on holiday or as a celebration cake.

Soak the currants in the sherry overnight.

Prepare a 25cm square cake tin by greasing and lining both base and sides with greaseproof paper. Fold just over a metre length of kitchen foil in half lengthways and half again and wrap round the outside of the tin. Hold in place with a length of string.

To make the cake, beat the butter and sugar together until pale and add the eggs, two at a time, mixing well with each addition. Add the currants, cherries and ground almonds. Sieve the mixed spice, baking powder, nutmeg and flour into the mixture. Stir well until completely mixed.

Bake at 160°C for an hour, then reduce the temperature to 150°C for a further 3 hours until baked. To test it is cooked through, insert a skewer and if clean it is done. If the top of the cake starts to brown too much cover with kitchen foil to prevent it browning further.

Allow to cool completely and then wrap well in greaseproof paper and tinfoil.

1.35kg (3lb) currants

2 wine glasses of sweet sherry

450g (1lb) butter

450g (1lb) caster (or brown) sugar

8 eggs

220g (8oz) glacé cherries

110g (4oz) ground almonds

560g (1¼lb) plain flour

1 teaspoon of baking powder

2 teaspoons of mixed spice

1 whole nutmeg (grated)

Yorkshire parkin

There are few things more delicious in a packed lunch than some well-matured parkin – richly flavoured, sticky and sustaining. It improves with keeping (if you can resist it!) so is great to take if you are going on a walking holiday.

Preheat the oven to 150°C. Put the oatmeal, flour and ginger in a large mixing bowl.

Melt the sugar, butter, syrup and treacle in a bowl in the microwave or a pan. Pour the melted ingredients into the flour with the eggs and milk and stir well.

Pour the mixture into a 30cm x 20cm tin lined with parchment paper. Bake for 45 minutes until brown but soft and sticky on top. Reduce the oven to 140°C and bake for a further 15 minutes.

Allow to cool then tightly wrap in parchment paper and clingfilm. For traditional parkin, store for a minimum of five days whilst it softens and matures.

340g (12oz) medium oatmeal

170g (6oz) self-raising flour

2 heaped teaspoons of ground ginger

170g (6oz) soft dark brown sugar

170g (6oz) butter

220g (8oz) golden syrup

60g (2oz) black treacle

2 eggs

120ml (4fl oz) milk

Gingerbread

This recipe for gingerbread is for a soft, light-textured cake not the old-fashioned firm, biscuit-type style. It is not as robust or filling as parkin but is so gingery and rich tasting – it is also popular served as a pudding with custard.

Preheat the oven to 150°C. Melt the margarine, sugar and syrup in a pan or in a bowl in the microwave.

Put the flour, bicarbonate of soda and ginger in a large bowl and mix together. Make a well in the centre of the flour and add the egg and gradually add the milk.

Add the melted sugar and beat well until you have a smooth, soft batter-like mixture. Pour into a 30cm x 20cm tin lined with baking parchment.

Bake in the centre of the oven for about 30 minutes until well risen and lightly firm to the touch. Try not to open the oven door during baking time as it may sink in the middle (if it does, continue to cook and serve as a pudding with custard).

140g (5oz) margarine

170g (6oz) dark soft brown sugar

220g (8oz) golden syrup

340g (12oz) self-raising flour

1 level teaspoon of bicarbonate of soda

2 heaped teaspoons of ground ginger

1 egg

200ml (7fl oz) milk

Swaledale view towards Muker from the foot of Buttertubs Pass

Doreen's Yorkshire spiced cheesecake

Yorkshire cheesecake is a local speciality and is unlike any other cheesecake you'll have tasted. The pastry base with a thin topping of spiced curd and dried fruit make a delicious addition to the tea table, contrasting well with sweeter sponge cakes.

Preheat the oven to 180°C. Sieve the flour and salt ino a bowl, and rub the lard and margarine in until it resembles breadcrumbs. Add the water, a little at a time, and stir with a knife until it is all combined. Grease a 20cm flan dish and line with the pastry.

Beat the butter and sugar together until pale and then add the egg and stir in. Add the cottage cheese, currants, flour and mixed spice to the mixture, stirring after each addition. Finally, add the rum or milk and stir until well combined.

Spoon into the pastry case and bake for 30 minutes until golden brown.

FOR THE PASTRY

220g (8oz) self-raising flour

Half a teaspoon of salt

60g (2oz) lard

60g (2oz) butter

4–5 tablespoons of cold water

FOR THE FILLING

60g (2oz) butter

60g (2oz) sugar

1 egg

220g (8oz) cottage cheese

85g (3oz) currants

30g (1oz) self-raising flour

1 teaspoon of mixed spice

3 tablespoons of rum (or milk)

Doreen's classic fruit scones

MAKES 12

Doreen's scones are famous throughout Swaledale and beyond. Over the years she reckons she will have made many thousands at the Auction Mart Café, funeral teas and countless functions around the Dale.

Preheat the oven to 200°C. Sieve the flour, baking powder and salt into a bowl. Using your hands, rub in the margarine and then add the sugar and currants, mixing well. Slowly add the milk, and stir in with a knife, until you have a soft dough.

Roll out on a floured surface to a thickness of about 2cm and cut with a 5cm-diameter cutter.

Place on a greased baking sheet and bake for 10 to 15 minutes until well risen and brown on top.

450g (1lb) self-raising flour

2 teaspoons of baking powder

A pinch of salt

85g (3oz) margarine

85g (3oz) caster sugar

85g (3oz) currants

About 150ml (¼ pint) milk to mix

Plain scones

MAKES 12

Straightforward, plain scones are delicious with homemade jam and whipped or clotted cream. You don't need the fruit to detract from the jam, or any butter as you have the cream. They also make up the topping for a classic cobbler pudding with stewed fruit such as rhubarb or gooseberries – a proper old-fashioned pud served with creamy custard (see page 187).

Preheat the oven to 200°C. Mix the flour, margarine and sugar together until you have an even, crumbly mixture. Add the eggs and slowly add the milk until the mixture is combined to form a soft but not sticky dough.

Turn the mixture out on to a floured surface and knead lightly to form a ball. Roll out into an oblong about 3cm thick and cut into 12 squares.

Place separately on a greased baking tray, leaving enough room for the scones to rise.

Bake for about 15 minutes, until golden brown, well risen and firm to the touch. Remove the scones from the baking tray on to a cooling rack.

450g (1lb) self-raising flour

170g (6oz) margarine

110g (4oz) caster sugar

2 eggs

About 150ml (¼ pint) milk

Wholemeal orange, date and walnut scones

MAKES 12

You can use all wholemeal flour for these, but it gives a lighter scone if you use half white self-raising flour. They will travel well if picnicking and will sustain you for a good afternoon's walking. If you don't like dates, just replace with juicy sultanas.

Preheat the oven to 200°C. Mix the flour, margarine and sugar together until you have an even, crumbly mixture. Add the nuts, dates and orange zest and stir. Add the eggs and slowly add the milk until the mixture is combined to form a soft but not sticky dough.

Turn the mixture out on to a floured surface and knead lightly to form a ball. Roll out into an oblong about 3cm thick, sprinkle with a little demerara sugar and cut into 12 squares.

Place separately on a greased baking tray, leaving enough room for the scones to rise.

Bake for about 15 minutes, until golden brown, well risen and firm to the touch. Remove the scones from the baking tray on to a cooling rack.

220g (8oz) wholemeal self-raising flour

220g (8oz) white self-raising flour

110g (4oz) margarine

110g (4oz) caster sugar

110g (4oz) walnuts, chopped

110g (4oz) chopped dates

Finely grated zest of an orange

2 eggs

About 150ml (¼ pint) milk

Demerara sugar to decorate

Traditional cheese scones

MAKES 12

These scones are light and really cheesy – use a good-quality mature Cheddar to give a rich flavour. They are unbeatable when eaten straight from the oven with a spread of cold butter.

Preheat the oven to 200°C. Mix the flour, margarine, mustard and cheese together until you have an even, crumbly texture. Add the eggs and slowly add the milk until the mixture is combined to form a soft but not sticky dough.

Turn the mixture out on to a floured surface and knead lightly to form a ball. Roll out into an oblong about 3cm thick. Sprinkle a small amount of milk on to the mixture and cover with the remaining cheese then cut into 12 squares.

Place separately on a greased baking tray, leaving enough room for the scones to rise.

Bake for about 15 minutes, until golden brown, well risen and firm to the touch. Remove the scones from the baking tray on to a cooling rack.

450g (1lb) self-raising flour

170g (6oz) margarine

Half a teaspoon of English mustard powder

220g (8oz) mature Cheddar cheese, grated, plus a small amount for the tops

2 eggs

About 150ml (¼ pint) milk

Traditional valley pastures, barns and walls at Gunnerside, Swaledale

Pesto and pinenut scones

MAKES 12

We once had this combination in the Seasons café in Richmond station and went straight home to experiment in the kitchen. The result was this deliciously tasty scone which is lovely on its own but makes a gorgeous base for an instant mini pizza – try them with either feta or cream cheese and rocket and cherry tomatoes.

Preheat the oven to 200°C. Put the flour, margarine, cheese and black pepper in a bowl and mix together. Add the pesto and pinenuts and mix again. Add the eggs and slowly add the milk until the mixture is combined to form a soft but not sticky dough.

Turn the mixture on to a floured surface and knead lightly to form a ball. Roll out into an oblong about 3cm thick and cut into 12 squares.

Place separately on a greased baking tray, allowing room to rise.

Bake for about 15 minutes until golden brown, well risen and firm to touch. Remove the scones from the baking tray on to a cooling rack.

450g (1lb) self-raising flour

85g (3oz) margarine

110g (4oz) mature Cheddar cheese, grated

Black pepper

110g (4oz) pesto

60g (2oz) pinenuts

2 eggs

About 150ml (¼ pint) milk

Easy chocolate brownies

MAKES 10–12

These are the quickest and most reliable chocolate brownies you will ever make – great for a picnic or teatime or a decadent pudding if served warm with local vanilla ice cream. If you can't eat nuts or for a children's picnic, stir a couple of packets of white chocolate buttons into the mixture before cooking. You can either melt the chocolate and butter together in the microwave (2 minutes on medium) or use a heat-proof bowl over a pan of simmering water.

Preheat the oven to 150°C. Melt the chocolate and butter together until smooth. Add all the rest of the ingredients and stir in well.

Put the mixture into a 30cm x 20cm baking tray lined with baking parchment.

Bake in the centre of the oven for approximately 35 minutes until risen and gently firm to the touch.

Leave to cool in the tin and cut into 10 to 12 pieces.

170g (6oz) butter or margarine

170g (6oz) good-quality dark chocolate

3 eggs

250g (9oz) caster sugar

140g (5oz) self-raising flour

110g (4oz) walnuts

A dessertspoon of Camp coffee or a teaspoon of instant coffee dissolved in a small amount of hot water

Honey and seed flapjack

MAKES 10–12

Elizabeth's mother adapted this recipe to make it more nutritious and interesting than ordinary flapjack. You can play around with it yourself – add some chopped dried apricots, cranberries or raisins, for example.

Preheat the oven to 160°C. Melt the margarine, sugar and honey in a pan or in a bowl in the microwave.

Off the heat, stir in the rest of the ingredients and mix well.

Put the mixture into a 30cm x 20cm baking tray lined with baking parchment.

Bake in the centre of the oven for approximately 30 minutes until golden brown and bubbling. Leave to cool in the tin and cut into 10 to 12 pieces.

110g (4oz) jumbo oats

110g (4oz) porridge oats

170g (6oz) margarine or butter

170g (6oz) demerara sugar

A large tablespoon of runny honey

110g (4oz) mixed seeds (sunflower, pumpkin and sesame)

Basic all-butter shortbread

MAKES 10–12

Simple to make in a hurry, stores well and a good staple in a lunch box.

Preheat the oven to 160°C. Mix all the ingredients together to form a fine crumb mixture and put in a 30cm x 20cm tin lined with baking parchment.

Level the mixture in the tin and press down lightly.

Bake for about 25 minutes until golden brown. Leave to cool and cut into 10 to 12 slices.

250g (9oz) plain flour

170g (6oz) butter

85g (3oz) caster sugar

Apricot crumble slice

Use good-quality, not-too-sweet apricot jam in this recipe, for a delicious crumbly slice. Alternatively, use chopped dates soaked in a little boiling water to soften, to make a paste to replace the jam.

Preheat the oven to 160°C. Make the shortbread as in the recipe on page 85 but remove from the oven after 15 minutes. Cool for about 10 minutes in the tin.

Spread the apricot jam over the shortbread.

Make the crumble topping by mixing together all the ingredients until you have a soft crumb. Sprinkle evenly over the jam. Sprinkle with flaked almonds, if required.

Bake for a further 20 minutes until golden brown. When cool, cut into 15 slices.

Basic all-butter shortbread (see page 85)

340g (10oz) jar of apricot jam

FOR THE CRUMBLE TOPPING

110g (4oz) plain flour

60g (2oz) porridge oats

85g (3oz) demerara sugar

110g (4oz) butter

Flaked almonds (optional)

The northern part of the Lake District near Blencathra and Skiddaw

Granny Perry's shortbread meringue

MAKES 15

Elizabeth's Grandpa Perry loved his food and was cuddly, rotund and adored by everyone who knew him. When no snacks could be found he would resort to the store cupboard for nuts, raisins and, particularly, glacé cherries. So we are very lucky that this recipe was ever made – it is a deliciously different addition to the tea table.

Preheat the oven to 160°C. Make the shortbread as in the recipe for all-butter shortbread (see page 85) but remove from the oven after 20 minutes.

In a large bowl, separate the eggs (put the egg yolks aside for lemon curd or egg custard tart) and whisk the whites to firm peaks. Gradually add the sugar until glossy and smooth. Add the cherries and walnuts and stir in gently.

Spread the meringue mixture on to the shortbread and return to the oven for a further 15 minutes. Allow to cool in the tin and cut into 15 slices.

Basic all-butter shortbread
(see page 85)

FOR THE TOPPING

2 egg whites

110g (4oz) caster sugar

60g (2oz) glacé cherries

85g (3oz) walnuts

CHIPPINDALE EGGS

Eggs have been in the press, often controversially, since the days of Edwina Currie and her salmonella scare in the mid 1980s. More recently, the questions have been more about production methods than the health benefits of the egg itself. Ethical practices and welfare issues have become important to the consumer.

Chippindale Foods is still sited on the family's original 20-acre smallholding at Kingsley Farm, near Harrogate, but whereas the original business was all about hatching chicks, keeping hens and selling eggs, today it is a far bigger enterprise. Nick and Lorna Chippindale are the third generation to run the company and have responded to the changing face of agriculture and demands from the consumer. Over the past few decades, they have become specialists in the grading, packing and distributing of eggs on behalf of a growing network of farmers across Yorkshire, the Humber and the North East. So although Chippindale Foods is now a very modern production company, there is nothing intensive about the way its eggs are produced – each individual farm is relatively small and, as a stand-alone unit would not necessarily be able to fulfil modern requirements but, having Chippindale's as a guaranteed buyer, they can remain profitable.

Nick's grandfather, Leonard, started the business in the 1930s and the enthusiasm for eggs in the family has remained undimmed. Nick's father started to diversify in the 1960s into packing eggs for Chippindale's and other farmers in the area. As a child, when Nick was growing up on the farm, one of his favourite pastimes was designing weird and wonderfully convoluted egg machines. He couldn't have known then that his inventions would contribute to the rapid growth in the company's fortunes. Today his egg machines offer complete traceability for customers and consumers.

2005 was the year Chippindale's introduced its groundbreaking online traceability tool: www.wheresyoursfrom.com. We love the fact that you can pick one of their eggs out of the box, log on to their website and see exactly which of the farms it came from. When chatting to Nick it becomes apparent that, to him, it is not whether the customer chooses to use the information or not but the fact that they can. By giving such transparency to the customer, quality and honesty become of utmost importance: it keeps everyone in the supply chain at the top of their game.

Now that the British Nutrition Foundation has said there are 'no limits' to the number of eggs you can eat, you can have them every day – fast food and good for you. Leonard Chippindale is testament to this, still enjoying a boiled egg for breakfast at 96 years old. Nick and Lorna usually get through at least a dozen a week. Their favourite is poached but their young children, Lottie, Alex and Ella, love it when Dad makes them a slice of eggy bread (see page 10).

Stephen Throup with one of his very happy free range hens

SUPPER

When you get back in after a long day out, whether it be from work, shopping or a day's walking, having a meal prepared is such a bonus. If you are having friends round or planning a special supper, it is worth making the effort in advance with something that just needs putting in the oven. Many casseroles can have all the hard work done beforehand and be left in the oven on timer to be ready when you walk through the door.

Food should look inviting, taste delicious and be made from the best ingredients available. It is always worth building a good relationship with your local butcher – he should always prepare meat to your requirements which makes life easier when you get it home. A reputable greengrocer will know the best vegetables available each week and even suggestions for cooking if you are unsure or want to try something new.

As busy working parents ourselves, we appreciate the need for convenience and speed. If you have had a roast chicken you can boil up the carcass to make a rich stock for soups and casseroles, but there's nothing wrong either with using good-quality stock cubes or vegetarian bouillon powder (just be a little cautious as some of them can be quite salty).

It's always worth spending the little bit extra to buy free-range eggs. They are a relatively inexpensive, very versatile ingredient and the fact that the hen leads a better life will make you feel better – likewise with chicken.

In our fridges, you will always find butter and milk, mature Cheddar cheese, soft cream cheese, ham, various vegetables and salads. On the side there is always a bowl of eggs and in the cupboard tins of tomatoes, sweetcorn, pasta and flour along with various herbs, spices and stock cubes. You are never far from a quick meal with those ingredients in store and they form the basis for many of our recipes.

Lastly, try not to be too rigid when following the recipes – try substituting different vegetables or herbs for variety and make recipes work individually to suit your personal tastes.

The northern Lake District landscape in the vicinity of Deer 'n Dexter's farm

BEEF

Good beef, like most meats, is best bought from your local butcher – even better if it comes from a farm in your area. Traditional butchers will allow the beef to hang for at least a couple of weeks or more, resulting in tender, full-flavoured meat. For mince, you don't want too much fat as it will make the resulting dish oily; but for steaks, for example, a good dark colour and some fat marbling through the meat will give a better result.

Gingered beef

SERVES 4

Everything about this dish is inviting, particularly the deliciously piquant smell. It works well with diced pork too. Serve with baked potatoes, rice or couscous and a green salad.

Put a large pan or casserole on the hob, on full heat. Add about a tablespoon of olive oil and the onion. Stir until softened and then add the garlic, chilli and ginger and stir for a further minute.

Add the beef and brown. Add the sugar, vinegar, tomatoes, pineapple and ginger beer.

Bring to the boil and stir well. Put the lid on the pan and either reduce the heat to minimum and simmer for 1¾ hours, or transfer to the oven preheated to 150°C for the same time.

The casserole does not need thickening and therefore is ideal for those with a gluten-free diet.

Olive oil

1 large onion, finely diced

1 teaspoon of chilli powder

A good piece of fresh root ginger, crushed or very finely diced

3 cloves of garlic, minced or very finely diced

1kg (2.2lb) chuck steak or shin of beef, diced

1 x 400g (14oz) tin of chopped tomatoes

1 x 340g (12oz) tin of pineapple chunks, in juice

110g (4oz) soft brown sugar

4 tablespoons of vinegar

A small bottle of strong ginger beer

Beef in Wold Top Brewery ale

SERVES 4 GENEROUSLY

This is a classic beef-in-ale casserole and makes a lovely meal, particularly in winter, served with spiced red cabbage, mixed root vegetables and either baked or dauphinoise potatoes. If you are going out for the day and want a meal ready for when you return, the casserole, cabbage and potatoes can all go into the oven on timer – what a welcoming aroma to greet you! If you prefer a beef-in-ale pie, just cook the meat following the recipe below, then transfer to a pie dish and top with puff pastry.

Soften the onion in the olive oil in a large pan or casserole on the hob, then add the garlic and meat. Stir until the meat is seared and then add the mushrooms and continue to cook for about 5 minutes.

Add the beer, stock cube, salt and pepper. Bring to the boil and stir well.

Put the lid on the pan and either reduce the heat to minimum and simmer for 1½ hours, or transfer to the oven preheated to 150°C for the same time.

Remove from the heat and thicken with the cornflour paste. Carefully stir on a low heat for a couple of minutes to cook the flour.

1 large onion, finely diced

Olive oil

2 cloves of garlic

1kg (2.2lb) chuck steak, diced

220g (8oz) mushrooms, sliced

A 500ml bottle of good beer, such as Wold Top Brewery ale

1 beef stock cube

Salt and black pepper

1 tablespoon of cornflour, mixed with water to make a thin paste

WOLD TOP BREWERY

A speciality beer, brewed in celebration of the nearby long distance Wolds Way footpath

It would seem that our nation loves its beer! In many areas of the food industry in the 1970s there was a move towards large scale production and economies of scale, resulting in the closure of many smaller businesses. The brewery industry was no exception. However, in the last decade or so there has been a revival in traditional brewing methods and micro breweries have sprung up around the country. Around the same time, the farming industry has had to adapt and many farmers have had to diversify to establish alternative sources of income to supplement their main activities.

Along the Coast to Coast route, there are a number of interesting micro breweries producing some excellent brews. Pat went to see Tom and Gill Mellor near the coast at Hunmanby who realised that their answer to the need to diversify was on their doorstep. Tom saw the same qualities that his grandfather had nearly 60 years before – the malting barley being grown, the fresh chalk-filtered water from a borehole sunk in the grassy dale – and the idea of the brewery came as an original and viable project that could be almost totally home grown and home made.

The farm already consisted of 600 acres of fertile soil as well as small dales and grazing areas and 20,000 free-range laying hens. Tom, along with neighbouring farmer Derek Gray, converted the old granary into a brewery. They spoke to nearby shops and pubs to see if there would be interest in a local brew and realised that there was a niche in the market, in this tourist orientated part of Yorkshire, for a local drink that originated right on the Wolds using grain and water from their own farms. Fortunately the businesses proved true to their word and the brewery developed a loyal base in the Scarborough, Bridlington and Beverley areas, stretching down the coast and inland.

The first beer to be produced was called Wold Top Bitter. Marketed as an easy drinking-session beer at 3.7 per cent, it proved popular (in fact, Tom says that even after six years and 12 other brews, this is still his favourite). It was followed by Falling Stone, a more rounded, smooth bitter. Interestingly, it is named after a meteorite which fell on the Grays' farm in 1795 and was so close to two farmhands that they were splattered with mud when it landed! The meteorite is now in the British Museum but there is a monument marking the spot where it hit the earth.

After this, Tom and Derek decided to name all their beers after local landmarks or events. Their pale ale was used by the National Trails Authority to celebrate the 25th anniversary of a walk which runs close by and in 2008 they introduced Centenary Way Mild to reflect the Centenary Way walk which runs through the farm.

Steak and kidney pie

SERVES 4 GENEROUSLY

This is so easy and quick to make, as well as being ideal for those who don't eat onions. You could add mushrooms. If you are really in a hurry, use half a packet of puff pastry for the top.

Put the meat in a large pan, pour the stock over and add salt and pepper. Bring to the boil, then reduce the heat to minimum, cover the pan and simmer for 1½ hours.

Remove from the heat and thicken with the flour paste. Stir on a low heat for a couple of minutes to cook the flour.

Transfer the meat to a suitably sized pie dish, keeping back some of the gravy.

Preheat the oven to 170°C. To make the pastry, put all the dry ingredients in a large bowl and stir together. Slowly add the water until the mixture binds together to form a ball (you can use a palette knife to start with so that it doesn't stick to your hands).

On a well-floured surface, roll out the mixture to a size to cover the pie dish. Brush with beaten egg. Bake in the oven for half an hour.

Serve with mashed potato, carrots and greens and the leftover gravy.

FOR THE FILLING

1kg (2.2lb) diced chuck steak and kidney

2 beef stock cubes dissolved in 600ml (1 pint) of boiling water

Salt and black pepper

30g (1oz) plain flour mixed to a paste in cold water

FOR THE PASTRY

110g (4oz) self-raising flour

110g (4oz) plain flour

110g (4oz) suet

Cold water

Salt and pepper

Doreen's meat pie

SERVES 2

Another of Doreen's classic recipes – her steak pies are legendary around the Dales and make an excellent family dinner on a winter's night.

Warm the oil in a frying pan. Roll the beef in the seasoned flour and brown in the oil. Put into a saucepan with the onion and the stock cube in water. Reduce the heat to minimum and simmer for 1½ to 2 hours until tender.

Place the meat in a small pie dish, approximately 15cm in diameter and 5cm deep, reserving the juices. Make the juice up to 1 pint with boiling water. To thicken, mix the cornflour and Bisto powder with a little cold water and add the juice to the mixture, stirring well. Pour back into the pan and bring to the boil, stirring continuously.

Pour about a quarter of the gravy over the meat in the dish and reserve the rest to serve with the pie.

Cover the pie with the shortcrust pastry and make a hole in the middle to let the steam out. Brush with beaten egg and bake at 190°C for 30 to 35 minutes until browned.

1 tablespoon cooking oil

340g (12oz) stewing or chuck steak, diced

Plain flour, seasoned with salt and pepper

1 small onion, finely chopped

1 beef stock cube, dissolved in 450ml (¾ pint) boiling water

1 tablespoon of cornflour

1 tablespoon of Bisto powder

170g (6oz) shortcrust pastry (170g plain flour, 85g butter, 85g lard, water)

Dexter cattle near Stoddah, Penrith

Traditional beef stew with horseradish and parsley dumplings

In this recipe, the dumplings give a Swiss roll effect which looks great if you have guests. If it is just the family, it is quicker and easier (but just as tasty!) to put all the dumpling ingredients in together and divide the mixture into five balls.

Put a large pan or casserole on the hob, on full heat. Add about a tablespoon of oil and the onion. Stir until softened and then add the meat.

Stir until the meat is seared and then add the carrots and stock. Bring to the boil and stir well. Put the lid on the pan and either reduce the heat to minimum and simmer for 1½ hours, or transfer to the oven preheated to 150°C for the same time.

Remove from the heat and thicken with the flour paste. Carefully stir on a low heat for a couple of minutes to cook the flour.

For the dumplings, put the flour, salt, pepper and suet in a mixing bowl. Slowly add the water until the mixture binds together to form a ball (use a palette knife to start with so that it doesn't all stick to your hands).

On a well-floured surface, you are now going to roll out the mixture into a rectangle of about 25cm x 20cm. Spread the horseradish sauce over the top and then sprinkle the parsley over, making sure you go right to the edges. Now carefully roll the dumpling mixture along the long length into a Swiss roll. Slice the roll into five equal pieces and place on top of the stew.

Put the lid back on the pan and return to the oven for a further half hour. Serve with creamy mashed potato and some greens.

FOR THE STEW

Vegetable oil

1 large onion, finely diced

1kg (2.2lb) chuck steak, diced

4 medium carrots, sliced

2 beef stock cubes dissolved in 600ml (1 pint) of boiling water

30g (1oz) plain flour mixed to a paste in cold water

FOR THE DUMPLINGS

220g (8oz) self-raising flour

110g (4oz) suet

Salt and pepper

Cold water

Horseradish sauce (about 2 tablespoons)

A good handful of fresh parsley, finely chopped

Doreen's braised steak with onions

SERVES 2

Braised steak is comfort food at its best. When you take the lid off the casserole there is melt-in-the-mouth beef in a rich, aromatic gravy – just made to be ladled over creamy mashed potato with some buttery cabbage and carrots.

Mix the flour with salt and pepper on a plate and roll the braising steak in it to coat completely.

Put the onion in a casserole dish, followed by the braised steak, and any flour mixture left.

Pour the stock, red wine, gravy browning and Worcester sauce over the meat.

Cover with a lid or cooking foil and cook at 150°C for 2 hours.

1 tablespoon of plain flour, seasoned with salt and black pepper

2 x 170g (6oz) braising steaks

1 medium onion, diced

2 teaspoons of gravy browning

1 beef stock cube, dissolved in 300ml (½ pint) of boiling water

3 tablespoons of red wine

1 teaspoon of Worcester sauce

60g (2oz) butter

Lasàgne

An all-year-round, popular dish which is a good family standby but also great for an informal supper with friends. A crunchy salad and some crusty or garlic bread, a bottle of red wine and the meal is ready.

In a large pan, soften the onion in the olive oil. Add the garlic and the mince and stir until the mince is browned. Add the tomatoes, purée and herbs. Stir well. When the mince comes to the boil, reduce the heat to minimum and cover the pan. Simmer for about 45 minutes.

While the meat is cooking, make the sauce. In a pan, melt the butter over a medium heat. Remove from the heat and add the flour. Mix to a paste and slowly whisk in the milk. Add the mustard and black pepper. Return to the heat and stir continuously until the sauce starts to thicken and come to the boil. Reduce the heat, continuing to stir for a further 2 minutes, to cook the flour. Remove from the heat and add the bulk of the cheese. Stir until the sauce is smooth and glossy.

Using a large, ovenproof dish, start to layer the lasagne. Put a quarter of the meat mixture on the bottom and arrange a layer of pasta sheets to cover. Do not overlap the pasta as it won't cook properly. Put another quarter of the meat on the pasta and top with about a quarter of the cheese sauce. Arrange another layer of pasta. Put another quarter of the meat on top and then another quarter of the sauce. Arrange another layer of pasta and top with the remaining quarter of meat and all of the remaining sauce.

Sprinkle the remaining cheese over the top and bake in the oven, preheated to 150°C, for an hour. When the pasta is cooked, the dish should be golden brown and bubbling and a knife can go straight through without resistance.

FOR THE FILLING

1 medium onion, finely diced

1 tablespoon of olive oil

2 cloves of garlic, crushed

500g (1.1lb) minced beef

2 teaspoons of mixed herbs

1x 400g (14oz) tin of chopped tomatoes, drained

1 tablespoon of tomato purée

Half a packet of lasagne pasta (about 12 sheets)

FOR THE CHEESE SAUCE

60g (2oz) butter

60g (2oz) plain flour

600ml (1 pint) milk

1 teaspoon of English mustard

Black pepper

170g (6oz) mature Cheddar cheese, grated, plus 60g (2oz) for the top

Shepherd's pie

A true British classic and so easy to eat if you're tired. Putting the carrots into the meat adds to the flavour and means you only need to prepare frozen peas to accompany it. The cheese on top gives an attractive bubbling finish when it comes out of the oven.

Put a large pan on the hob, on full heat. Add the oil and onion. Stir until softened and then add the meat.

Stir until the meat is browned and then add the carrots and stock. Bring to the boil and stir well. Put the lid on the pan, reduce the heat to minimum and simmer for about 45 minutes.

When cooked, stir in the flour paste and continue to stir for a couple of minutes to cook the flour. Put into a pie dish.

For the mash, put the prepared potatoes in a large pan and cover with water. Cover the pan and bring to the boil. When boiling, reduce the heat and simmer until soft. Drain and add the butter, milk and salt and pepper. Mash thoroughly until smooth.

Put the mash on top of the mince and lightly fork it out to cover. Sprinkle with the cheese and bake in the oven at 180°C for about 20 minutes until golden brown.

A tablespoon of oil

1 large onion, diced

1kg (2.2lb) minced beef

4 carrots, sliced

1 beef stock cube, dissolved in 300ml (½ pint) of boiling water

1 tablespoon of plain flour mixed with water to make a paste

4 good-sized potatoes, peeled and cut into four

Venison casserole

Obviously venison is not beef, but this is too good a recipe to miss out. In the past few years, venison has become much more readily available and is no longer considered a meat only served in stately homes. This special casserole would be a welcome centrepiece for any dinner party. Serve with new potatoes, spiced red cabbage and wilted spinach.

Preheat the oven to 150°C. On the hob, soften the onions in the olive oil and butter in a large casserole dish. Add the garlic, bacon and mushrooms and continue to cook for a further 5 minutes. Add the venison and brown the meat.

Next add the red wine, port, stock, bay leaves, redcurrant jelly and salt amd pepper. With a potato peeler, peel the zest off the orange and add to the casserole (you will remove it later) and then squeeze the juice and add it.

Bring to the boil and stir well. Put the lid on the casserole and place in the middle of the oven for 2 hours.

Remove from the oven and place over a low heat on the hob. Take out the bay leaves and the orange zest. Stir well and add the cornflour paste a little at a time until the gravy is thickened. Continue to stir to cook the flour for a couple of minutes.

Decorate each plate with a sprig of rosemary and a bunch of fresh redcurrants, if available.

2 medium onions, diced

1 tablespoon of olive oil

30g (1oz) butter

4 cloves of garlic, finely chopped

4 rashers of smoked bacon, chopped

450g (1lb) mushrooms, sliced

1.2kg (2.5lb) haunch or shoulder of venison, diced

Half a bottle of good, full-bodied red wine

1 glass of port

1 beef stock cube, dissolved in 300ml (½ pint) of boiling water

2 bay leaves

3 tablespoons of redcurrant jelly

Salt and black pepper to taste

Zest and juice of an orange

About a tablespoon of cornflour, made into a paste with cold water

6 strands of redcurrants to decorate

6 sprigs of rosemary to decorate

DEER AND DEXTER AT OLD STODDAH FARM

Old Stoddah Farm sits in the Lake District under the imposing mountain of Blencathra. Nothing can quite prepare you for the contrast between the rugged, harsh landscape of the area and the total tranquillity felt when watching the deer quietly grazing.

The striking thing about this farm is the way the animals are naturally and non-intensively reared. They are bred exactly as they would be in the wild, from mating, giving birth and weaning. The deer and cattle enjoy a diet of grass and herb-rich pasture, provided by the surrounding hills and valleys. The grassland is kept organic with no addition of fertilisers. As they are grass-fed rather than cereal-based, the animals grow more slowly, giving a more tender and flavoursome meat.

Jane Emerson and Peter Stoeken started their farm in a very small way in 1987, expanding as they were able. As their backgrounds were in forestry and landscaping, when the opportunity came up to realise their long-held dream of having their own smallholding, deer seemed a natural way forward. They felt that the landscape and climate were perfectly suited to rearing deer in the Lakes.

From the outset they wanted their animals to live a natural life. The stock roam in a safe natural environment with plenty of space and lots of shelter from the wind and rain as well as shade on the occasional sunny day. They are checked daily and that level of contact means that Jane and Peter know the individual animals and the animals trust them. To minimise stress and maximise quality, the farm has its own small slaughterhouse as well as butchery.

Each year, Jane and Peter rear about 125 calves, which are born from May to July and stay with their mothers until the autumn, a natural weaning point. Some of the calves from each season are selected as replacements for breeding, thereby sustaining the herd and reducing the biosecurity risks associated with introducing animals from outside.

Over the past few years, with increasing awareness of the benefits of a healthy diet, venison has become a much more popular choice of meat. It is a very good source of protein, while, unlike most meats, it tends to be fairly low in fat, especially saturated fat, and is rich in iron and important vitamins and minerals. Whilst it is still considered relatively expensive, it is so rich and flavoursome that a smaller quantity is required.

In 2003, Jane and Peter decided to diversify away from just deer and, after much consideration, introduced Dexter cattle to their farm. About half the size of modern commercial cattle, the breed's small stature and hardy nature means they are well suited to thriving in the harsher climate of the Lake District. Jane and Peter apply the same high welfare standards to the rearing of the Dexters as they do to the deer. The beef produced tastes like beef as it did in the old days, with natural marbling and depth of flavour.

Part of Deer 'n Dexter's deer herd

LAMB

How to decide which joint is best for a Sunday dinner – shoulder of pork with crispy crackling; a really well- hung sirloin or rib of beef; or a succulent, plump roast chicken? However, tender, melt-in-the-mouth leg of lamb is hard to beat, particularly when accompanied by freshly made mint sauce.

Lamb is an easy meat to cook and gives rise to a wide variety of dishes. You can have new-season lamb chops ready within 10 minutes in a hot oven or can leave a shoulder of lamb hotpot to cook in a low oven for 3 hours – some of the Middle Eastern dishes can even be left to cook for over 12 hours. Lamb is delicious with nothing more than a little salt on the skin but is equally well married with a range of aromatic spices.

Roast leg of lamb with garlic and rosemary   SERVES 6

Roast leg of lamb is delicious with nothing more than a light brush of oil and a sprinkle of sea salt, but it's also enhanced by the addition of some garlic and rosemary. Serve with crispy roast potatoes, cauliflower cheese and carrots or roasted root vegetables – not forgetting some homemade mint sauce on the side. It is a combination that never fails to please all those around the table, especially when accompanied by a rich red wine.

To make mint sauce, finely chop a good handful of freshly picked mint and mix it with 30g (1oz) caster sugar dissolved in a little boiling water and 2 tablespoons of malt vinegar. Stir well. Adjust sweetness to taste.

Preheat the oven to 200°C. With a sharp knife, make six deep cuts into the flesh of the leg of lamb and, using your index finger, push the rosemary sprigs and some garlic into each one. Rub the lamb all over with a little olive oil and sprinkle with coarse sea salt.

Place the lamb into a roasting tin and put in the middle of the oven. After 20 minutes, reduce the heat to 180°C and cook for a further 1½ hours.

Remove from the oven and transfer to a clean dish, cover with foil and leave to sit for at least 15 minutes to relax the meat.

Put the roasting tin, with the juices from the meat, on to the hob at a medium heat. Add the flour and thoroughly stir into the juices. Remove from the heat and slowly whisk in the stock, plenty of black pepper and a good pinch of salt, making sure you get all of the sticky cooked bits from the bottom of the pan. Put the pan back on the heat and bring up to boil, stirring continuously.

2kg (4.4lb) leg of lamb

6 sprigs of fresh rosemary

6 cloves of garlic, cut into chunky slivers

Olive oil

Coarse sea salt

30g (1oz) plain flour

1 beef or lamb stock cube, dissolved in 600ml (1 pint) of boiling water

Black pepper

One-pot lamb shanks

This recipe came from Elizabeth's mother, Margaret Baker, who is a classic country cook. It cooks beautifully in a large pot on top of a stove – even a camping stove – and is even more flavoursome on reheating.

Toss the shanks in the plain flour until coated. In a large pan or casserole, fry the shanks in olive oil until sealed and browned. Put to one side.

In the juices, soften the onions and carrots until lightly coloured and then add the fennel, butternut squash, peppers and garlic. Reduce the heat and continue to cook for 10 to 15 minutes to develop the flavours.

Put the lamb back into the pan with the vegetables and add the wine. Season to taste. Place the sprigs of thyme on top of the meat.

Cover the pan and reduce the heat to minimum. Leave to simmer for 3 hours. Alternatively, cook in the oven at 150°C for 45 minutes and then reduce the heat to 130°C for a further 2¼ hours.

Boil the new potatoes for 15 minutes and add to the casserole for the last half hour of cooking.

4 lamb shanks

Plain flour

Olive oil for frying

2 large onions, diced

2 carrots, peeled and diced

1 bulb of fennel, sliced

1 small butternut squash, peeled and diced

2 red peppers, deseeded and sliced

6 cloves of garlic, finely chopped

Half a bottle of full-bodied red wine

Salt and black pepper to taste

4 large sprigs of fresh thyme (wild thyme if available)

1kg (2.2lb) washed new potatoes

Summer lamb hotpot

This is a much lighter version of traditional hotpot, made with chicken stock, and is so delicious that you will want some bread to mop up all the gravy. It keeps in the fridge for a few days and freezes well. If you want to make this dish for a special occasion, you can use chops instead of diced meat. Serve with green vegetables such as garden peas, baby broad beans or runner beans.

Preheat the oven to 150°C. In a large casserole dish, seal the meat in the olive oil. Put to one side.

Add the butter to the pan and soften the onion. Return the meat to the pan with the onion.

Cut the tops off the carrots and wash well but do not peel. If the carrots are little, leave them whole, but if they are larger cut them in half and add to the pan with the potatoes, thyme and stock. Season with black pepper and a little salt and bring to the boil.

Put the lid on the casserole and cook in the oven for 1½ hours.

Thicken with the cornflour paste and stir for a further 5 minutes on the hob to cook the flour. Sprinkle with the chopped parsley before serving.

Either 700g (1.5lb) diced shoulder of lamb or 8 lamb chops

1 tablespoon of olive oil

1 large onion, diced

30g (1oz) butter

1 bunch of carrots with their tops on, or small new-season carrots

12 new potatoes, scrubbed

2 chicken stock cubes, dissolved in 900ml (1½ pints) of boiling water

A few sprigs of thyme

Salt and black pepper

2 tablespoons of cornflour, dissolved in cold water to make a paste

A good handful of parsley, finely chopped

BELL'S OF GILLGATE

There are so many good farmers in the Dales producing premium-quality meat in a traditional way. As the daughter of a Dales farmer, born and brought up in Wensleydale, Pat knows many of the farmers personally but chose to visit the Bell family of Gillgate Farm because, as part of their farm development, they offer an online direct-marketing service of their lamb and mutton. Gillgate Farm is now run by brothers Bruce and Stephen Bell with the next generation of James and also Ian who helps with marketing and sales. The family have been farming near Askrigg for over 200 years and still follow many of their great-grandfather James Scarr's original methods, set in place in the 1800s. As with many farms in the area, Gillgate is a mixed dairy and sheep farm. The herd of 80 cows produces milk for the production of Hawes Wensleydale cheese and they have a sheep flock based on 1,000 pedigree Swaledale ewes.

Twenty years ago, when you could still kill animals on the farm, Elizabeth's father used to supply friends down country with home-reared lamb. They were universally judged to be the 'best lamb ever tasted'. He was interested in researching the feasibility of a small-scale abattoir based at Hawes, in order to market Wensleydale lamb in the same way as the Welsh marketed theirs. He was convinced that the lean, flavoursome, tender meat was comparable if not superior to Welsh lamb and should command an equally dominant position in the market. Ironically, it took the horrors of foot and mouth disease in 2001 and the realisation of the detriment to animal welfare due to the distances travelled to be slaughtered for there finally to be an abattoir in Upper Wensleydale.

Sheep in Wensleydale near Hawes

Why is the lamb so good? As you walk the Coast to Coast route, you will notice the herb-rich meadows and pastures, as well as the heather-covered moorland, both of which provide grazing for the lambs. Gillgate sells its lambs throughout the year with individual eating qualities changing according to the season. The small number of spring lambs, traditionally eaten at Easter, are from the faster-maturing continental Texel breed and are born in February. They are wholly milk and grass reared, resulting in succulent, tender meat. The first of the main crop of lambs are out of the more hardy indigenous Swaledale ewes and are reared on the herb-rich pastures and flower meadows which give a full-flavoured, richer meat. Possibly the sweetest, purest flavour of any of the lamb comes from the heather-fed sheep; straight off the moors, they are characterised by small, lean lamb chops from which some say that you can smell the purple heather as it cooks. They are the nearest thing to wild lamb, being left to graze with their mothers on the heather and mountain grasses. The last to be sold are the autumn lambs which, due to their maturity, have a deeper flavour; although they are larger animals, the meat is still succulent and tasty.

In 2007, in response to customer demand, the Bells made mutton available for the first time in many years from Gillgate. For centuries, mutton was the staple meat of the British household, considered superior in texture and flavour to lamb. However, for the last 50 years mutton supply has declined and it almost disappeared from our shops and restaurants. A mutton renaissance campaign was launched in 2004 by the Prince of Wales to support British sheep farmers who were struggling to sell their older animals. The campaign has been a great success and mutton is now back on the menu.

Doreen's lamb casserole

SERVES 4

This is a quick casserole to prepare and really flavoursome to eat.

Preheat the oven to 150°C. Roll the lamb in the seasoned flour and place in a casserole dish together with any remaining flour.

Add the onion, carrots, white wine and lamb stock. Put the lid on the dish and cook for 1½ hours.

Remove from the oven and add the apricots, butter beans, mint jelly and redcurrant jelly (if the gravy is not thick enough add some gravy granules) and cook for a further half hour.

700g (1½lb) diced shoulder of lamb

1 tablespoon of plain flour, seasoned with salt and black pepper

1 medium onion, finely diced

2 carrots, sliced

300ml (½ pint) white wine

1 lamb stock cube, dissolved in 300ml (½ pint) of boiling water

12 dried apricots

1 x 400g (14oz) tin of butter beans

2 tablespoons of mint jelly

2 tablespoons of redcurrant jelly

Northern Lakes above Bassenthwaite Lake

Lamb's liver with smoked bacon and onions

SERVES 4

You either love or hate liver! People who loathe it tend to have memories of liver in gravy for school dinners – little bullets of strong-tasting meat, so tough and dry you can barely swallow it. Liver is an economical meal, is very high in iron and other minerals and is packed with vital vitamins. If pan-fried with onions and bacon, with the gravy made in the pan and eaten soon afterwards, it is a quick and tasty meal – a true winter warmer. Try this recipe on your family and you will convert them. Do buy fresh lamb's liver, not pig's liver which has a different taste and texture altogether.

In a large frying pan, brown the onion in the oil over a medium heat. Add the bacon and continue to stir until it is cooked. Remove the onion and bacon from the pan and set aside.

Mix a good pinch of salt and some black pepper into the flour in a bowl. Cover the liver in flour and fry in the pan for about 2 to 3 minutes on each side (depending on the thickness of the meat) over a high heat, until brown. You will probably need to do this in two batches, putting it with the onion and bacon whilst cooking the second batch.

Reduce the heat to low and add the remaining flour to the pan. Stir well to absorb any juices and then slowly add the beef stock, whisking well to mix in any lumps.

Put the liver, bacon and onion back in the pan and simmer gently for about 10 minutes.

Serve immediately with mashed potato and buttered cabbage.

1 medium onion, sliced

1 tablespoon of vegetable oil

4 rashers of smoked bacon, cut into small strips

1 tablespoon of plain flour

Salt and black pepper

700g (1½lb) fresh lamb's liver, sliced into thin strips (the butcher will do this)

1 beef stock cube, dissolved in 300ml (½ pint) of boiling water

Elizabethan lamb

Elizabeth first made this recipe for a TV programme about food from around the UK when filming at Bolton Castle in Wensleydale where Mary, Queen of Scots was imprisoned in the 1500s. It's now something of a signature dish and is unfailingly popular with friends. Due to the spices, it is a casserole that marinates if kept for a couple of days in the fridge, so can be prepared well in advance. It freezes perfectly so is a great standby meal for unexpected visitors. Serve with couscous and a green salad.

In a casserole dish, soften the onions with a small amount of olive oil. Add the chilli, garlic, ginger and ground coriander and continue stirring for a further minute while the spices cook.

Add the lamb and brown the meat. Add the apricots, raisins, wine, stock and honey. Stir well and bring to the boil.

Put the lid on the casserole dish and either simmer gently on the hob or place in the oven at 150°C for 1½ hours.

Remove from the oven and put on the hob on a medium heat. Add the cornflour paste, a little at a time, until the casserole is thickened. Continue to stir for a couple of minutes to cook the flour.

Stir in the chopped coriander and serve immediately.

2 medium onions, finely chopped

Olive oil

A large thumb-sized piece of root ginger, peeled and finely chopped

2 small red chillis, finely chopped, or 2 teaspoons of chilli powder

6 cloves of garlic, very finely chopped

2 teaspoons of ground coriander

1.3kg (3lb) diced lamb (ask your butcher for a mixture of shoulder and leg)

110g (4oz) raisins

110g (4oz) apricots, chopped

Half a bottle of white wine

300ml (½ pint) chicken stock or a chicken stock cube, dissolved in 300ml (½ pint) of boiling water

A tablespoon of runny honey

30g (1oz) cornflour, dissolved in a small amount of cold water to make a paste

A good handful of chopped coriander

Spiced squeaky lamb pie

SERVES 4

This is a delicious alternative to the traditional shepherd's pie and something a bit different if you are going for easy entertaining. The spices add warmth to the meat and the cabbage in the potato gives a lovely taste and texture like the old-fashioned bubble and squeak.

In a pan, soften the onion in a small amount of olive oil. Add the garlic, chilli, ginger, coriander and cumin and continue to stir for a minute to cook the spices. Add the mince and stir until the meat is browned. Add the apricots, sultanas and stock.

Put a lid on the pan, reduce the heat to minimum and simmer for 45 minutes.

Whilst the meat is cooking, boil the potatoes in a pan until soft. Drain and mash with the butter, cream and salt and pepper.

Bring a pan of salted water to the boil and add the cabbage. Rapidly boil for 2 minutes (no longer as the cabbage will continue to cook in the oven). Drain immediately and add to the mashed potato.

When the meat is cooked, add the cornflour paste a little at a time, until the sauce is thickened.

Put the meat into an ovenproof dish and top with the mashed potato. Sprinkle with the cheese, if required, and put into the oven, preheated to 170°C, for about 15 minutes until golden brown and bubbling. If you are making the pie in advance, it will need to go into a preheated oven at 170°C for about 40 minutes to heat through.

1 medium onion, finely diced

Olive oil

3 cloves of garlic, finely chopped

Half a red chilli, deseeded and finely chopped

A 3cm piece of root ginger, peeled and finely chopped

1 teaspoon of ground coriander

1 teaspoon of ground cumin

900g (2lb) minced lamb

110g (4oz) dried apricots, chopped

85g (3oz) sultanas

1 chicken stock cube, dissolved in 150ml (¼ pint) of boiling water

4 potatoes, peeled

2 tablespoons of double cream

30g (1oz) butter

Salt and black pepper

Quarter of a savoy cabbage, finely sliced

1 tablespoon of cornflour, made into a paste with cold water

60g (2oz) mature Cheddar cheese, grated (optional)

CHICKEN

Never mess around with roast chicken – just keep it simple with a crispy, salty skin and succulent meat. It is the perfect centrepiece to a traditional roast dinner but also a great accompaniment to risotto or salad and new potatoes in summer. For an easy, but absolutely delicious, picnic, take a basket with a freshly roasted chicken (wrap the roasting tin in a tea towel to keep it warm, keeping the buttery juices for dipping bread in), some cherry tomatoes, mayonnaise, black pepper and crusty baguettes. Add some homemade lemonade and chocolate brownies (see page 82), and you will have some very happy friends.

Perfect roast chicken

SERVES 4–6

1.2kg (2.5lb) chicken, preferably free range

60g (2oz) butter, softened

About a teaspoon of fine sea salt

You will need a roasting tin and some parchment paper. Line the bottom of the roasting tin with a piece of parchment paper that is long enough to come back up and over the bird. Put the chicken in the tin and rub the body and legs with butter. Sprinkle evenly with salt. Bring one end of the paper up over the bird and then fold the other end over it. Tuck firmly down the sides of the chicken.

Place in the middle of the oven, preheated to 180°C. Roast for about 1¼ hours and then fold back the paper to reveal the breast of the chicken and continue to roast for a further 10 minutes, until it is golden brown.

If you have a temperature probe, the meat should be above 75°C. If you don't have one, prod the meat with a skewer at the bottom of the leg and the juices should run clear.

If you are not serving the chicken straight away, it should either be chilled down to below 5°C or eaten within 90 minutes.

Chicken in a smoked bacon and mushroom sauce   SERVES 4–5

This is a very popular, easy recipe to make and delicious to eat. If you are looking for a lower-fat option, stir in some reduced-fat crème fraîche instead of cream and reduce the amount of butter in the sauce. Serve with rice or new potatoes and side salad.

Preheat the oven to 170°C. Cut the chicken into strips (about eight per breast) and put into an ovenproof dish. Dot with half of the butter and cover with parchment paper. Bake in the oven for 20 minutes until cooked.

While the chicken is cooking, prepare the sauce. In a pan, soften the onion with the remaining butter, add the bacon and then the sliced mushrooms. Stir until softened. Add the chicken stock and bring up to the boil.

When the chicken is cooked, put it into the sauce with all the juices from the dish. Reduce the heat and simmer for 5 minutes, then add the cornflour paste.

Just before serving, add the cream and stir well.

4 chicken breasts

60g (2oz) butter

1 medium onion, finely diced

4 rashers of smoked bacon, cut into lardons

220g (8oz) mushrooms, sliced

1 chicken stock cube, dissolved in 300ml (½ pint) of boiling water

1 tablespoon of cornflour, dissolved in a little cold water to make a paste

150ml (¼ pint) double cream

Cogill Beck above Gillgate

Chicken in an orange and ginger sauce

SERVES 4–5

We love this way of serving chicken – really zingy with a kick of ginger and it is almost totally fat free. Serve with rice, couscous or new potatoes and side salad.

Preheat the oven to 170°C. Cut the chicken into strips (about eight per breast) and put into an ovenproof dish. Sprinkle with a little olive oil and cover with parchment paper. Bake in the oven for 20 minutes until cooked.

While the chicken is cooking, prepare the sauce. In a pan, soften the onion with the olive oil and then add the garlic, root ginger and ground ginger. Stir for a couple of minutes before adding the orange juice and stock. Bring to the boil then reduce the heat and simmer for 10 minutes to allow the ginger to infuse.

Take the chicken from the oven and add it to the sauce, with the juices from the dish. Add the cornflour paste and orange segments and stir well. Continue stirring for a further couple of minutes to cook the flour.

4 chicken breasts

1 medium onion, finely diced

1 teaspoon of olive oil

A good piece of fresh root ginger (a fat thumb size), peeled and very finely chopped or crushed

1 level teaspoon of ground ginger

2 cloves of garlic, very finely chopped or crushed

Juice of 3 large oranges or 300ml (½ pint) of freshly squeezed juice

1 chicken stock cube, dissolved in 150ml (¼ pint) of boiling water

1 large orange, segmented without pith

1 tablespoon of cornflour, dissolved in a little cold water to make a paste

Thai-style chicken

SERVES 4

This is such a deliciously flavoured, gently spiced, creamy dish. It almost certainly bears no relation to authentic Thai-style chicken, but with the coconut, lime and coriander it certainly tries. Serve with rice.

Preheat the oven to 170°C. Slice the chicken breasts into strips and place in an ovenproof dish, dot with half the butter and cover with parchment paper. Bake in the oven for 20 minutes until cooked through.

While the chicken is cooking, prepare the sauce. In a pan, soften the onion with the remaining butter and then add the garlic, chilli, ginger and ground coriander. Stir for a couple of minutes, then add the stock and coconut cream. Bring to the boil then reduce the heat and simmer for 15 minutes to infuse. Add the cornflour paste with the lime zest and juice.

Remove the chicken from the oven and stir into the sauce with the juices from the dish. Stir in the chopped coriander leaves and then the cream.

4 chicken breasts

60g (2oz) butter

1 small onion

2 cloves of garlic, very finely chopped or crushed

1 red chilli, deseeded and finely chopped

A 3cm piece of fresh ginger, peeled and finely chopped

1 teaspoon of ground coriander

85g (3oz) coconut cream

1 chicken stock cube, dissolved in 200ml (7fl oz) boiling water

Zest and juice of a lime

2 teaspoons of cornflour, dissolved in a little cold water to make a paste

A good handful of fresh coriander, chopped

150ml (¼ pint) double cream

Chicken and mushroom pie

This pie uses roast chicken rather than chicken breasts. Firstly, it is cheaper, but also more flavoursome. You can make this recipe using pastry or with a mashed-potato topping. Serve with peas and carrots.

After roasting the chicken, set to one side to cool for at least half an hour before handling it.

Pour off the juices from the roasting tin into a large pan. Add the mushrooms and cook on the hob until softened. Remove from the heat and stir in the flour. Slowly add the milk and then the chicken stock. Return to the heat and stir continuously until the sauce thickens and comes to the boil. Reduce the heat and continue to cook for a further 2 minutes.

Preheat the oven to 180°C. Strip all the meat off the chicken, breast and legs. Cut into bite sized pieces and put into the sauce.

Make the pastry by rubbing the fat into the flour and binding with cold water until it forms a smooth ball. Roll out half of the pastry just larger than the pie dish and use to line the base. Put the chicken mixture on to the pastry. Brush the edges of the pastry with beaten egg, roll out the remaining pastry and use to cover the top of the pie. Cut round the edges and press to seal.

Cut some leaves out of the remaining pastry. Brush the pie with beaten egg and arrange the leaves on top. Brush the leaves with egg. Cut a couple of small slits in the centre of the pie to allow any air to escape whilst cooking.

Bake in the centre of the oven for 45 minutes. Serve with mashed potato, peas and carrots.

FOR THE FILLING

1.2kg (2.5lb) chicken, roasted (See page 115)

220g (8oz) mushrooms, sliced (or the same weight of ham if preferred)

60g (2oz) plain flour

300ml (½ pint) milk

1 chicken stock cube, dissolved in 300ml (½ pint) of boiling water

FOR THE PASTRY

280g (10oz) plain flour

85g (3oz) lard

110g (4oz) butter

Cold water

Chicken and potato pie

This is a delicious variation on a chicken pie. It is substantial and filling so it doesn't need any more than some fresh green vegetables and carrots or a salad to serve with it.

Finely slice the potatoes like crisps. Melt the butter in a frying pan and soften the onion. Add the sliced potatoes and stir into the buttery onion. Continue to cook the potatoes for about 15 minutes, stirring occasionally to avoid them sticking to the pan. Put the potatoes into a bowl with the thyme leaves.

Cut the chicken into strips and seal in the frying pan. Add to the potatoes. Season the chicken and potatoes with plenty of black pepper and half a teaspoon of salt.

Preheat the oven to 180°C. Make the pastry by rubbing the fat into the flour and binding with cold water until it forms a smooth ball. Roll out half the pastry just larger than the pie dish and use to line the base. Put the chicken and potato mixture on to the pastry and press down. Brush the edges of the pastry with beaten egg, roll out the remaining pastry and use to cover the top of the pie. Cut round the edges and press to seal.

Cut some leaves out of the remaining pastry. Brush the pie with beaten egg and arrange the leaves on top. Brush the leaves with egg. Cut a small circle out of the middle but leave in place.

Bake in the centre of the oven for half an hour. Remove the circle of pastry in the middle of the pie and slowly add the cream. Replace the circle and put the pie back in the oven for a further 20 minutes. Allow to sit for 10 minutes before serving.

FOR THE FILLING

4 large potatoes, peeled

110g (4oz) butter

1 medium onion, finely diced

1 dessertspoon of fresh thyme leaves

3 large chicken breasts

Salt and black pepper

150ml (¼ pint) double cream

FOR THE PASTRY

280g (10oz) plain flour

85g (3oz) lard

110g (4oz) butter

Cold water

Beaten egg to glaze

Stuffed chicken breasts

A stuffed and wrapped chicken breast is easy to prepare, can be done well in advance and looks impressive at the table. They are equally good if thinly sliced and served cold to make a lovely addition to a picnic.

Allow one breast and a couple of rashers of bacon or pancetta per person. If you can get hold of pancetta or another cured thinly sliced bacon, it does give a crispier texture to the finished dish. All you need to do is lay the two slices of bacon flat on a preparation board, to form a kind of blanket for the chicken. Put the chicken breast on to the centre of the bacon and cut a slit along the length of it, not quite cutting all the way through. Now you can fill the chicken with the stuffing of your choice and firmly pull the bacon up round it. Secure with a wooden cocktail stick if needed or turn the chicken over so that the bacon ends are underneath. Bake in the oven, preheated to 170°C, for about 40 minutes until browned and bubbling. As it cooks, the chicken and stuffing make a lovely sauce which is delicious drizzled over potatoes or salad.

Chicken liver and orange or Blue Wensleydale and walnut pâté (see page 56) work really well as stuffing, but, if you are in a hurry, a good-quality pâté from a deli will do just as well. Alternatively, slices of mozzarella cheese with cherry tomatoes and thyme is good or slices of Stilton with walnuts. Doreen uses a combination of Wensleydale cheese and soft cheese with garlic and herbs. Experiment with your own fillings and discover your own favourites.

Rich grazing west of Reeth

Chicken and broccoli pie

This is a favourite in Elizabeth's family and very popular with all the children's friends too. It is easily prepared in advance and has broccoli and potatoes already in the pie, so perfect for a quick supper after a busy day, served simply with carrots.

After roasting the chicken, set to one side to cool for at least half an hour before handling it.

1.2kg (2.5lb) chicken, roasted (see page 115)

Pour off the juices from the roasting tin into a large pan. Add the flour to the pan and stir until combined. Slowly add the milk and the stock cube. On a medium hob, stir the sauce until it thickens and comes to the boil. Set aside.

60g (2oz) plain flour

450ml (¾ pint) milk

1 chicken stock cube

For the mash, put the prepared potatoes in a large pan and cover with water. Cover the pan and bring to the boil. When boiling, reduce the heat and simmer until soft. Drain and add the butter, milk and salt and pepper. Mash thoroughly until smooth.

4 good-sized potatoes, peeled and quartered

60g (2oz) butter

A good dash of milk

Preheat the oven to 180°C. Cut the broccoli into small florets. In a pan, pour over enough boiling water to cover and boil rapidly for 2 minutes. Drain and set aside.

Salt and black pepper

A good-sized head of broccoli

Strip all the meat off the chicken, breast and legs. Cut into bite-sized pieces and put into the sauce then add the broccoli. Put the chicken mixture into a pie dish and top with the mashed potato.

Dot the top of the pie with butter and bake in the oven for 30 minutes until golden brown.

Mild chicken curry

A quick and easy recipe which isn't in any way authentic, but is popular with adults and children alike. Whilst the chicken is cooking, put the rice on the stove, the naan breads in the oven, make an easy cucumber relish and, within half an hour, you've made your dinner.

Put the rice in a large pan, add the salt and cover with water until the level is twice as deep as the rice. Bring to the boil and then reduce the heat to simmer for about 20 minutes.

In another pan, soften the onion in the oil and then add the garlic. Add the spices and continue to stir for a further minute. Remove from the heat.

In a frying pan, lightly fry off the chicken until golden brown and then add to the spices in the other pan. When all the chicken is cooked, stir well and add the chicken stock and milk. Bring to the boil and then reduce the temperature to minimum and simmer for 10 minutes.

Whilst the chicken is cooking, cut up the cucumber and mix with a small pot of yoghurt, the chopped mint and a squeeze of lemon juice. Stir well together and put into a serving bowl.

Put the naan breads in the oven to warm through.

Add the cornflour paste to the chicken and stir for a couple of minutes to cook the flour. Put into a dish and sprinkle with the almonds, sultanas and coriander. Drain the rice and serve.

220g (8oz) basmati rice

1 level teaspoon of salt

1 tablespoon of olive oil

1 medium onion, finely diced

3 cloves of garlic, finely chopped

2 tablespoons of medium curry powder

2 teaspoons of ground cumin

4 chicken breasts, cut into strips

1 chicken stock cube, dissolved in 300ml (½ pint) of boiling water

300ml (½ pint) milk

Half a cucumber, finely chopped

A good handful of fresh mint, very finely chopped

150ml (¼ pint) tub of natural yoghurt

A squeeze of lemon juice

Naan breads (available from most supermarkets)

1 tablespoon of cornflour, dissolved in a little water to make a smooth paste

Flaked almonds, sultanas and chopped coriander, to serve

PORK

Pork is probably the least popular of all meats but, when cooked well, really can be the most delicious. When you cook a joint of pork shoulder, no one can walk past without trying to pinch a little of the crunchy, salty crackling. Choose a shoulder rather than leg, as the fat coursing through the meat gives a much more tender and full-flavoured joint. To get good crackling every time, just rub the scored rind with a little vegetable oil and sprinkle with a generous quantity of salt. Preheat the oven to 210°C and place the pork on the middle shelf for 25 minutes. Turn the oven down to 150°C and continue to cook for the necessary time (a 2.5kg joint will take about 2 hours).

Pork with apples and Calvados

SERVES 4–5

This is Elizabeth's mother's recipe from the days when she served dinner to bed and breakfast guests in Askrigg – she was renowned for her fabulous food and this is one of her popular dishes that's relatively easy to make. Try to use a good pressed apple juice – it really makes a difference, especially if you can get a slightly sharp one, such as a Bramley. Serve with dauphinoise potatoes, carrots and spiced red cabbage.

Preheat the oven to 150°C. In an ovenproof casserole dish, soften the onion in the oil. When soft, add the garlic and continue to stir for a further minute. Add the meat and seal.

Warm a tablespoon on the hob and pour the Calvados brandy on to it. Carefully light the brandy using a match and tip it into the casserole. Repeat with another spoonful (if you don't burn off the alcohol, it can be a little sharp in the finished dish).

Add the apples, apple juice, stock cube, salt and pepper. Bring to the boil and then transfer to the oven for 90 minutes.

After cooking, remove from the oven and put back on the hob over a low heat. Add the cornflour paste and continue to stir for about 5 minutes to cook the flour. Add the cream just before serving.

1 medium onion, diced

1 teaspoon of olive oil

2 cloves of garlic, very finely chopped

1kg (2.2lb) diced shoulder of pork

2 tablespoons of Calvados apple brandy

2 Cox's apples, peeled, cored and sliced

1 Bramley apple, peeled, cored and sliced

1 chicken stock cube

600ml (1 pint) good pressed apple juice, such as Luscombe or James White

Salt and black pepper to taste

1 tablespoon of cornflour, dissolved in a little water to make a paste

150ml (¼ pint) double cream

Pork with cider and Cox's apples

SERVES 4

This recipe was adapted from the one on page 125. It is more economical to make and, because it has no cream, is a lower-fat version – perfect for a less formal supper or for the family. It is delicious served with baked or mashed potato, greens and carrots.

In an ovenproof casserole dish, fry off the onion in the oil until soft. Add the diced pork and seal the meat.

Add the apples, apple juice, stock cube and salt and pepper. Bring to the boil and then transfer to the oven, preheated to 150°C, for about 90 minutes.

Remove from the oven and put back on to the hob over a low heat. Add the cornflour paste and stir for about 5 minutes to cook the flour.

1 large onion, diced

1 teaspoon of olive oil

1kg (2.2lb) diced shoulder of pork

2 Cox's apples, peeled, cored and sliced

1 Bramley apple, peeled, cored and sliced

1 chicken stock cube

600ml (1 pint) good pressed apple juice, such as Luscombe or James White

1 tablespoon of cornflour, dissolved in a little water to make a paste

Salt and black pepper

Urra Moor on the Cleveland Way

Quick pork and chicken cassoulet

SERVES 4

Cassoulet is such a sociable meal as, once it is prepared, the hard work has been done. It is packed with flavour and is a true meal in a bowl, needing little more than some crusty bread or a simple salad. This recipe uses small pieces of pork with chicken and tinned beans, so it can be ready in 1½ hours. If you can't get hold of chorizo, use four spicy fresh sausages, cut them into four and fry them with the pork. The beauty of this casserole is that it will sit and wait quite happily if you are not ready to eat as quickly as you expected. It also freezes well or keeps in the fridge for a couple of days.

Preheat the oven to 150°C. In a large casserole dish, brown the chicken and pork in the olive oil and then set aside.

Soften the onion, garlic and peppers in the meat juices.

Put the meat back in the pan with the sausage, beans, tomatoes, purée, herbs and stock. Season with salt and black pepper and stir well.

Bring to the boil, then cover the dish and cook in the oven for 1½ hours until the meat is tender.

4 chicken thighs (skin on)

280g (10oz) diced shoulder of pork

1 tablespoon of olive oil

1 large onion, diced

4 cloves of garlic, finely diced

2 red peppers, deseeded and sliced

110g (4oz) chorizo sausage, cut into chunks

2 x 400g (14oz) tins of haricot beans

1x 400g (14oz) tin of chopped tomatoes

1 tablespoon of tomato purée

2 tablespoons of chopped fresh herbs, such as thyme, oregano, rosemary

300ml (½ pint) of chicken stock or 1 chicken stock cube dissolved in 300ml (½ pint) of boiling water

Salt and black pepper

Boiled gammon with sweet and sour sauce

SERVES 4

Always get a bigger piece of gammon than you need for this meal, as home-cooked ham is unbeatable for delicious, chunky sandwiches with pickle the following day. You can find prepared pieces of gammon in most supermarkets but, if you are buying from the butcher, ask him to tie it firmly, to keep the joint whole while cooking. A larger (2.5kg) piece of ham will only add about half an hour to the cooking time of a smaller (1.5kg) piece. The sauce is quick and easy to make. You can prepare it well in advance and any left over will freeze beautifully for a quick supper another day. For a real comfort meal, serve with mashed potato and broccoli or peas.

In a large enough pan to fit the joint, cover the gammon with cold water. Bring to the boil, put the lid on the pan and simmer gently for 2 hours (or put in an oven, preheated to 150°C, for the same time).

Drain the water from the joint. Allow to sit for about 10 minutes and then carve into 1cm-thick slices, as required.

To make the sauce, soften the onion in the oil over a medium heat and then add the garlic. Stir for about a minute before adding the pepper and mushrooms. Cook until the mushrooms are softened. Add the tomatoes, purée, sugar, vinegar, sweetcorn and pineapple.

Bring to the boil and then reduce the heat and simmer for about 30 minutes. Add the cornflour paste and stir for about 5 minutes to cook the flour.

Pour the sauce over the slices of hot ham.

1.5kg (3lb) uncooked gammon joint

1 medium onion, finely diced

1 teaspoon of olive oil

2 cloves of garlic, very finely chopped

1 red pepper, cored, deseeded and sliced

8 mushrooms, sliced

1x 220g (8oz) tin of chopped pineapple with juice

1x 220g (8oz) tin of sweetcorn

2 tablespoons of demerara sugar

4 tablespoons of malt vinegar

1 x 400g (14oz) tin of chopped or baby tomatoes

1 tablespoon of tomato purée

1 tablespoon of cornflour, dissolved in a little water to make a paste

Mashed potato-topped sausage pie

This family favourite is popular with both children and adults and is a great one for students as it is economical to make, filling and tasty. You can also add a tin of baked beans to the mixture for extra bulk and texture. Serve with peas and sweetcorn.

Preheat the oven to 180°C. Peel the potatoes and boil until soft. Drain. Add the butter and a pinch of salt and black pepper and mash, adding milk or cream until you have a creamy texture.

Roll the sausage meat into walnut-sized balls and place in an ovenproof pie dish. Put in the oven and bake for 15 minutes until sizzling but not brown.

While the meat is cooking, put the onion in a pan with the olive oil and cook until softened. Add the tomatoes, purée, herbs, salt and pepper and bring to the boil. Simmer for a good 20 minutes to reduce the sauce. Pour over the cooked sausage balls.

Top with the mashed potato and sprinkle with grated cheese if required. Return to the oven for 30 minutes until golden brown.

4 large potatoes

30g (1oz) butter

Salt and black pepper

2 tablespoons of double cream or milk

1kg (2.2lb) good sausage meat, preferably from your butcher as it is not as fatty (you could use thick sausages and cut them in half)

1 medium onion, diced

1 tablespoon of olive oil

2 x 400g (14oz) tins of chopped tomatoes, drained

2 tablespoons of tomato purée

2 teaspoons of mixed herbs

60g (2oz) mature Cheddar cheese, grated (optional)

Slightly spicy pork balls with spaghetti

SERVES 6

This is an easy and inexpensive recipe to make and can be prepared and cooked in a short time so is great when you have a quantity of people waiting to be fed. We have made the pork balls slightly spicy, but you can leave out the spices and just have them plain.

Start by making the sauce. In a large saucepan, fry off the onion in a little olive oil until it is softened and golden brown. Add the garlic and continue to stir for a further minute, whilst the garlic softens. Add the tomatoes, purée, paprika and salt and pepper. Reduce the heat to minimum and cook the sauce for about 30 minutes.

To make the meatballs, put all the ingredients in a large bowl and mix together thoroughly. Put a frying pan on the hob with a little oil. Get a bowl of clean, cold water and dampen your hands (this makes it easier to mould the pork balls). Now roll enough mince between your palms to make walnut-sized balls and put them in the frying pan. Keep turning the balls over until they are golden brown and cooked through, then remove from the pan and add to the sauce. Repeat until all the mince is used up.

Meanwhile, follow the instructions on the packet and cook enough spaghetti for everyone. When the spaghetti is cooked, drain and divide on to plates and put the meatballs and sauce on top.

Sprinkle with some chopped basil or another herb of your choice.

FOR THE MEATBALLS

1kg (2.2lb) minced pork

110g (4oz) fresh breadcrumbs

2 teaspoons of chilli powder

1 teaspoon of ground ginger

Half a teaspoon of freshly grated nutmeg

Salt and black pepper to taste

FOR THE SAUCE

1 onion, finely diced

Olive oil

2 cloves of garlic, finely chopped

1 x 400g (14oz) tin of chopped tomatoes

1 tablespoon of tomato purée

2 teaspoons of paprika

Salt and black pepper to taste

Dried spaghetti, cooked in salted boiling water (usually about 40g dry weight per person)

View down onto village of Muker

FISH

Although we live in the middle of the countryside, we have access to some great fresh fish through two excellent fishmongers who visit the local markets. We always have fillets of salmon and cod or haddock in the freezer, as they are so quick to thaw out, giving a meal within half an hour if you have nothing prepared. Sustainability of fish stocks is always in the news and we owe it to future generations to be cautious when buying fish, checking the source is a reputable one. The health benefits of fish are well documented and it should play a regular part in our diet.

Fish pie

This pie, with chunks of succulent fish and creamy mashed potato on top, is true comfort food. You can vary the fish according to what is in season, on offer or just what your family enjoy. The lemon juice in the sauce cuts down the level of salt but, as an alternative, you can replace the lemon juice and parsley with 170g (6oz) of mature white Cheddar. If you want a lower-fat option, use 60g of cornflour, made into a paste with a little milk, and add it directly to the milk in which you poached the fish, eliminating the need for butter and plain flour – this is also then suitable for those following a gluten-free diet.

Put the fish into a saucepan with the milk and bring to just under boiling point. Turn off the heat immediately, put a sieve over a jug and pour off the milk. Arrange the fish in an ovenproof dish.

In a pan, melt the butter with the flour and then, off the heat, slowly whisk in the milk from the jug, making a smooth sauce. Return to the heat and whisk constantly until the sauce is thickened and boiling. Remove from the heat and add black pepper, parsley and lemon juice. Pour the sauce over the fish.

In a pan, boil the potatoes for about 20 minutes until soft and then mash with the cream, butter and salt.

Cover the top of the fish and sauce with the mashed potato and top with the cheese, if required.

Put the pie in the oven, preheated to 170°C, for about 20 minutes until golden brown and bubbling. Serve with peas.

450g (1lb) mixed fish
(salmon, cod, haddock)

300ml (½ pint) milk (skimmed or full fat)

60g (2oz) butter

60g (2oz) plain flour

A good handful of fresh parsley,
finely chopped

Juice of a lemon

Black pepper

4 large potatoes, peeled and
cut into quarters

30g (1oz) butter

2 tablespoons of double cream or milk

A pinch of salt

60g (2oz) mature Cheddar cheese

Salmon en croute

SERVES 4

Fish is most often associated with lemon but this dish has a subtle hint of orange which complements the salmon beautifully. Serve it with a selection of salads and new potatoes, and it can be eaten cold if you are wanting a smart dish for an open-air concert or picnic.

Preheat the oven to 200°C. Firstly, zest the orange and set aside for the filling. Cut the salmon pieces in half, horizontal to the surface of the chopping board, giving thin slices of fish. Squeeze the orange and put the juice in a bowl with the salmon.

Cut the pastry in half and roll out one half to give a rectangle about 20cm x 10cm. Prick the pastry all over with a fork to help it to rise evenly. Bake in the oven for about 15 minutes until well risen and golden brown.

Whilst the pastry is cooking, prepare the filling. In a pan, melt the butter over a medium heat and fry the spring onions until softened. Rinse the spinach and add to the pan. Stir until the spinach has withered and shrunk back into the pan. Drain off any excess liquid and allow to cool. When cool, add the orange zest, soft cream cheese, a pinch of salt and black pepper. Mix together thoroughly.

When the pastry is cooked, drain the orange juice off the salmon. Use half of the fish to totally cover the pastry. Put the spinach filling on top of the fish and spread it out evenly. Use the rest of the salmon to cover the spinach, creating a sandwich effect. Now roll out the remaining pastry to a large enough rectangle to completely cover the fish and pastry base (this will be a similar size to the original piece as the base will have shrunk when cooking).

Beat an egg in a small dish and brush around the edge of the cooked pastry base. Lay the rolled-out pastry over the fish and gently tuck it under the base, pressing carefully to seal the en croute. Make a few small slits in the top of the pastry to allow air to escape whilst it is cooking. Use the beaten egg to glaze the pastry by brushing all over. If there is any spare pastry, you could cut out leaves or small fish shapes to decorate by sticking them on top of the dish.

Bake in the oven for 15 minutes and then reduce the heat to 170°C and bake for a further half hour until golden brown and well risen.

Zest and juice of an orange

4 salmon portions

1 x 500g pack of chilled puff pastry

30g (1oz) butter

4 spring onions, sliced into 1cm pieces

Half a large bag of fresh spinach

110g (4oz) soft cream cheese

Salt and black pepper

Egg to glaze

Plaice with prawns in a cheese sauce

SERVES 4

This is a very simple dish to make but looks really inviting. You can either serve it in one large dish or in individual gratin dishes. Accompany with peas and some new potatoes in summer or creamy mash in winter.

Preheat the oven to 170°C. Grease the dish with butter. With a fillet of fish skin side up in the dish, place a quarter of the prawns at the wider end of the fillet. Carefully roll the fish over the prawns and continue rolling fairly firmly until you have a Swiss roll effect. Turn the fish so that the end of the fillet is on the bottom. Repeat with the rest of the fillets.

To make the cheese sauce, melt the butter in a pan, over a medium heat. Remove from the heat and stir in the flour. Gradually whisk in the milk and return to the heat. Bring to the boil, stirring frequently to stop the sauce sticking to the pan and burning. Continue to stir for a further couple of minutes to cook the flour. Remove from the heat and add the bulk of the cheese. When the cheese is melted and you have a smooth sauce, pour the sauce evenly over the fish. Sprinkle the remaining cheese on top and bake in the oven for 30 minutes until golden brown and bubbling.

4 small to medium fillets of plaice

110g (4oz) prawns

30g (1oz) butter

30g (1oz) plain flour

600ml (1 pint) milk

160g (6oz) mature Cheddar cheese, grated, plus 60g (2oz) for the top

Half a teaspoon of English mustard powder

A good grind of black pepper

Sauces for fish

The following sauces can be served with most fish, including salmon, cod, haddock or plaice. They are delicious with creamy mashed potato, peas and spinach but work just as well for a lighter dish in summer with salad and new potatoes. To poach fish, put the fish in a pan of cold water with a pinch of salt and a tablespoon of lemon juice and bring to just under boiling point. Turn off the heat and leave in the hot water for about 5 minutes until opaque and cooked through. To oven cook, preheat the oven to 170°C and place the fish on a piece of parchment paper in an ovenproof dish, with a dot of butter and a squeeze of lemon juice. Cover the dish with foil and bake for about 20 minutes until cooked.

Light prawn and lemon sauce

SERVES 4

This is a quick and easy sauce which is lower in fat than the cheesy sauce opposite and, because it uses cornflour, is a good alternative for those with a wheat intolerance.

Put the cornflour in a pan and slowly whisk in the milk. Add a good grind of black pepper and a pinch of salt and bring to the boil over a medium heat. Reduce the heat to minimum and continue to stir for a further couple of minutes to thicken the sauce. Remove from the heat and add the prawns and lemon juice. Pour over the fish and bake, covered with foil, for about 20 minutes until the fish is cooked.

60g (2oz) cornflour

600ml (1 pint) skimmed milk

Salt and black pepper

110g (4oz) prawns

Juice of a lemon

Doreen's hollandaise sauce

SERVES 4–6

Slowly melt the butter in a saucepan. Put the white wine vinegar and lemon juice in another saucepan and bring to the boil. Blend the egg yolks and salt in a food processor then, keeping the processor running, slowly add the white wine vinegar and lemon juice, followed by the hot melted butter. Keep the processor running while the sauce thickens. Serve immediately.

170g (6oz) butter

1 tablespoon of white wine vinegar

2 tablespoons of lemon juice

3 egg yolks

Pinch of salt

Sunset on Solway Firth

RAY'S SHRIMPS OF SILLOTH

Nothing quite illustrates the diversity of produce available in the UK better than the natural harvest from the seas – shrimps in abundance from the cold, shallow tidal bays of the west coast, yet cross over to the east coast and herrings are the staple product. Both are totally sustainable in their area and produced without any need for intensive methods.

Shrimps have been taken from the bays around our coasts for centuries and Pat went to visit Ray's Shrimps, a family-run business operating out of Silloth, on the beautiful Solway Coast. Silloth faces the hills of southern Galloway and is backed by the Lake District fells. Well known for its sea views and glorious sunsets, the town was planned as a railhead and port in the 1850s. Victorians visited for the health benefits of clean air and sea bathing, and from that era Silloth boasts a large promenade and spacious green areas on the seafront. More recently it claims to have one of the best links golf courses in the country, which helps to keep it a popular holiday destination today.

Ray's Shrimps was founded by the late Alan Ray and his wife Joan in the early 1960s. It is still a family-run concern today, with their son Joe, daughter Julie and grandson Jason managing the business. The whole process, from fishing to cooking, packing and potting, is handled by the family who are all passionate about what they do.

The shrimps from the bay are brown shrimps which differ from their more available pink cousin, the prawn. They have a much meatier texture and a lot more flavour than the prawn,

Shrimp boats in the Solway Firth at Silloth; Dumfries and Galloway coast on horizon

making them delicious to eat on their own without the need for sauces and dressings. They are caught using sustainable fishing methods by the Rays' own boats, the *Jolanda* and the newly acquired *Solway Provider*, cooked on board in fresh seawater, landed and then transported to the newly fitted processing unit adjacent to the dock. Although there is a nod to modern methods of processing, the end product is as pure and additive free as it was hundreds of years ago. Instead of a group of 'pickers' de-shelling the shrimps by hand, as would have happened until recently, the shrimps are graded for size and put through shrimp-peeling machines before being inspected to remove any little pieces of shell. They are then either vacuum packed or potted. The potting of both fish and meat, one of the oldest-known preservation methods, has been practised for centuries. By covering potted food with fat, the air is excluded so the storage life is extended. At first, ingredients were cooked in a pot, cooled and then covered with a thick layer of suet, but by Tudor times butter had replaced the suet.

Ray's use a traditional recipe and method, originally adopted by the Silloth Shrimp Company, which supplied Young's at Annan in the 1950s. The shrimps are added to hot spiced butter, cooked then drained, weighed into pots and 'sealed' with a good-quality farmhouse butter.

More recently, to respond to changing consumer tastes, Ray's introduced a garlic potted shrimp. These are cooked in garlic butter with black pepper and parsley and sealed with more fresh garlic butter. They are a convenient little pot to have in the fridge for a quick and easy lunch – warm with crusty bread or with a baked potato. For supper, just sprinkle the warmed shrimps over a pan-fried piece of salmon or fillet of white fish for a simple yet delicious meal.

Parsley and lemon sauce

Make this in the same way as the prawn sauce, but instead of prawns add a good handful of finely chopped parsley. This is ideal for pouring over fish steaks and a good alternative in a fish pie.

Doreen's mushroom sauce

Mushroom sauce is so handy for fish, steaks or pork chops. This is Doreen's version – you could add a little wholegrain mustard to pep it up a bit with meat.

Melt the butter in a saucepan, then add the mushrooms and coat with the butter. Add the flour, stir well until it is smooth and then add the milk a little at a time. Keep stirring until the sauce thickens. Season to taste.

60g (2oz) butter

110g (4oz) mushrooms, chopped or sliced

1 tablespoon of plain flour

300ml (½ pint) milk

Salt and pepper

Fishing village of Staithes, near Whitby

Traditional fish cakes

SERVES 4

This recipe makes two good-sized fish cakes per person. Serve with salad in summer or potatoes, carrots, peas and parsley sauce in winter.

Firstly, you need to cook the fish. Cook in the way described on page 136. If you have got the oven on anyway, you might as well use the heat. However, it may be more economical to quickly poach it on the hob. Remove the fish from the water using a slotted spoon.

Boil the potatoes for about 20 minutes and drain thoroughly. When the potatoes are cold, mash them with a fork and then add the fish, a pinch of salt, lots of freshly ground black pepper, the parsley and lemon juice.

To make the cakes, separate the mixture into the size of cake that you need and roll it between the palms of your hands to make a ball shape. Push your hands lightly together to compress the ball. Carefully roll the cake in the beaten egg and then cover with breadcrumbs.

In a frying pan, melt the butter and oil together until bubbling and then fry the fishcakes for 5 minutes on each side until golden brown.

450g (1lb) white fish (cod, haddock, coley, etc)

450g (1lb) peeled weight of potatoes

A good handful of chopped parsley

Juice of a small lemon

Salt and black pepper

Beaten egg

2 slices of white bread, made into crumbs

30g (1oz) butter

A tablespoon of vegetable oil

The Fish Quay in Whitby Harbour

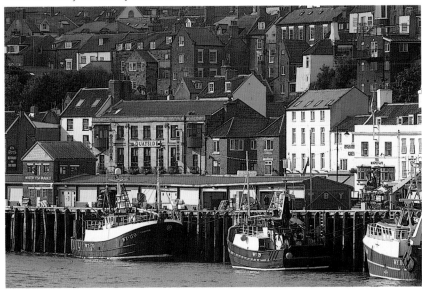

Salmon and spring onion fish cakes

SERVES 4

The inspiration for these cakes came from making the salmon en croute on page 134. The orange works so well with the fish and these fish cakes are just a little richer than the traditional ones, making them ideal for when you want something a bit special.

Cook the fish and potatoes as for traditional fish cakes on page 141.

Soften the spring onions in a little bit of butter either in the microwave or in a pan on the hob over a medium heat.

In a bowl, mash the potatoes and then add the salmon, orange zest, cream cheese, spring onions, a pinch of salt and plenty of freshly ground black pepper. Mix together thoroughly.

Now shape the mixture into cakes and fry as described for traditional fish cakes – you should have enough mixture for eight good-sized cakes.

340g (12oz) salmon fillet, skinless and boneless

340g (12oz) peeled weight of potatoes

4 spring onions, cut into 1cm pieces

1 tablespoon of full-fat cream cheese

Zest of an orange

Salt and black pepper

Beaten egg

2 slices of bread, made into crumbs

Whitby at Sunrise

Spiced crab cakes

SERVES 2 AS A MAIN COURSE OR 4 AS A STARTER

If you are lucky enough to be on holiday or live by the sea, particularly in Cornwall or Norfolk, you will be able to get fresh crab from the local fishmonger. The white meat is perfect for sandwiches but for fish cakes you really need the full flavour which comes from using the brown meat as well. These fish cakes are more expensive to make, but they are so delicious and rich that you don't need them to be too big.

Boil the potatoes until soft and drain thoroughly.

In a small pan, over a medium heat, gently cook the garlic, ginger and chilli in the oil.

In a bowl, mash the potatoes and then add the crab, garlic and spices. Mix together thoroughly, then add the coriander and stir in.

Divide the mixture into the size you require and shape into fish cakes, as described for traditional fish cakes.

Fry in a frying pan with a little butter and oil for 5 minutes on each side until golden brown and crispy.

110g (4oz) peeled weight of potatoes

2 teaspoons of olive oil

2 cloves of garlic, peeled and crushed

2cm piece of fresh root ginger, peeled and grated

Half a red chilli, deseeded and very finely chopped

1 medium dressed crab

A tablespoon of chopped fresh coriander

Beaten egg

1 slice of bread, made into crumbs

VEGETARIAN DISHES

When we're asked to cater and provide two dishes, with one suitable for vegetarians, many people ask for a little taster of the vegetarian one. These meals are so full of flavour, inviting colours and texture that they will go down well with family and friends, whether traditional meat eaters or not.

Spiced sunny bean pie

SERVES 6

The flavours in this recipe work really well together and the 'sunny' top from the sweet potatoes makes it look very appetising. You can soak the beans overnight if you have them or you can use tinned ones for speed and convenience.

In a large casserole soften the onion in the oil. Add the garlic, ginger, chilli and red pepper and stir for a couple of minutes. Add the beans, chick peas and lentils with the tomatoes and purée. Season well with salt and plenty of freshly ground black pepper. Reduce the heat to minimum and cover the pan. Simmer gently for 40 minutes until the lentils are soft and the sauce reduced and thickened.

While the lentils are cooking, prepare and boil the potatoes (do this in two separate pans as the sweet potatoes take less cooking). When the potatoes are cooked, mash together with the butter, cream, salt and pepper.

Put the bean mixture in the bottom of a large ovenproof dish and top with the mashed potato. Sprinkle the top with the cheese and bake in the oven at 170°C for about 20 minutes until golden brown and bubbling (if reheating from cold, it will need around 40 minutes).

Serve with a salad or green vegetables such as spinach or broccoli.

FOR THE FILLING

1 large onion, chopped

1 tablespoon of olive oil

4 cloves of garlic, finely chopped

A large thumb-sized piece of ginger, peeled and finely chopped

1 red chilli, deseeded and finely chopped

1 red pepper, deseeded and sliced

1x 400g (14oz) tin of haricot beans

1x 400g (14oz) tin of kidney beans

1 x 400g (14oz) tin of chick peas

110g (4oz) green lentils, rinsed in cold water

1 x 400g (14oz) tin of chopped tomatoes

2 tablespoons of tomato purée

Salt and black pepper

FOR THE POTATO TOPPING

3 large potatoes, peeled and cut into quarters

3 sweet potatoes, peeled and cut into quarters

2 tablespoons of double cream

60g (2oz) butter

Salt and black pepper

60g (2oz) mature Cheddar cheese, grated

View down onto fertile Vale of Mowbray between the North York Moors and Yorkshire Dales

Lentil pancake stack

This lentil mixture is really useful and can be used where non-vegetarians would use mince, as in lasagne or shepherd's pie. You can bulk it up by adding courgettes, aubergines or butternut squash with the peppers. It keeps well in the fridge and is a useful standby in the freezer. In this recipe, we have put it between pancakes to make a layered dish which you slice like a cake, with a tangy cheese sauce over the top. Serve with a mixed salad or roast tomatoes.

Start by making the pancake batter. Put the flour, salt and pepper in a large bowl and crack the eggs into the middle with a little of the milk. With a whisk, start to mix the eggs and milk into the flour, forming a thick paste. Slowly add the rest of the milk, whisking thoroughly until you have a single-cream consistency. Set aside for half an hour whilst you make the lentil filling.

In a pan, soften the onion in the oil, then add the garlic and peppers and stir for a further couple of minutes. Add the lentils, tomatoes, purée, herbs, stock, a pinch of salt and a good grind of black pepper. Bring to the boil and then reduce the heat to minimum. Cover the pan and allow to simmer gently for 45 minutes, stirring occasionally.

To make the cheese sauce, melt the butter in a pan over a medium heat. Remove from the heat and add the flour. Mix to a paste and slowly whisk in the milk. Add the mustard and black pepper. Return to the heat and stir continuously until the sauce starts to thicken and come to the boil. Reduce the heat, continuing to stir for a further 2 minutes, to cook the flour. Remove from the heat and add the cheese. Stir until the sauce is smooth and glossy.

Next make the pancakes. Heat a frying pan over a medium heat with a little oil to stop the pancakes sticking to the pan. Pour in enough batter to just coat the bottom of the pan and swirl it round to cover it evenly. When the underside is golden brown, carefully turn it over and cook the other side (use a palette knife to help lift the edge). Turn the pancake out on to a plate and make up the rest.

FOR THE PANCAKES

110g (4oz) plain flour

Salt and black pepper

2 eggs

300ml (½ pint) milk

FOR THE LENTIL FILLING

1 medium onion, finely chopped

2 cloves of garlic, very finely chopped

1 tablespoon of olive oil

2 peppers, preferably red and yellow, deseeded and chopped

220g (8oz) brown or green lentils, rinsed in cold water

1 vegetable stock cube, dissolved in 150ml (¼ pint) of boiling water

1 x 400g (14oz) tin of chopped tomatoes

2 tablespoons of tomato purée

2 teaspoons of mixed dried herbs or 2 tablespoons of chopped fresh herbs

Salt and a good grind of black pepper

To put the dish together, use a buttered dish, wider than the pancakes. Put a pancake on the bottom of the dish and spread enough lentil mixture to cover the pancake. Put another pancake on top of the lentils and repeat the process until you have used all eight pancakes, leaving the top one uncovered. Pour the cheese sauce over the pancake stack and top with the rest of the cheese.

If the stack is still warm, bake in the oven, preheated to 160°C, for 20 minutes until golden brown and bubbling. If cooking from cold, preheat the oven to 150°C and bake for about 35 minutes until heated through.

FOR THE CHEESE SAUCE

30g (1oz) butter

30g (1oz) plain flour

450ml (¾ pint) milk

1 teaspoon of English mustard

Black pepper

140g (5oz) mature Cheddar cheese, grated, plus 60g (2oz) for the top

Lis's cannellini bean and vegetable pie

SERVES 6

Lis owns our local chemist's in Hawes and gave this recipe to Doreen to use at Butt House.

Soak the beans overnight in plenty of water, then drain and rinse.

Melt two-thirds of the butter in a saucepan and fry the onion until it is soft. Add the beans, garlic and water and bring to the boil. Simmer gently for 1 hour, until the beans are soft and the liquid reduced to a thick sauce. Stir in the tomato purée and basil and season with salt, pepper and sugar.

Meanwhile, cook the potatoes and mash with the remaining butter and a little milk, then season to taste. Cook the carrots and leeks.

Grease a casserole dish and put the carrots and leeks in before pouring over the bean mixture. Sprinkle with half of the cheese then spread the mashed potato on top. Lightly fork over and sprinkle with the remaining cheese.

Bake at 190°C for 30 to 40 minutes until crispy and golden on top.

170g (6oz) cannellini beans

60g (2oz) butter

1 large onion, finely chopped

2 cloves of garlic, finely chopped, or 1 teaspoon of garlic purée

450ml (¾ pint) water

2 tablespoons of tomato purée

Half a teaspoon of dried basil

Salt and black pepper

1 teaspoon of sugar

700g (1½lb) potatoes, peeled and diced

Milk

450g (1lb) carrots, diced

450g (1lb) leeks, sliced

110g (4oz) grated cheese

Doreen's stuffed peppers

SERVES 2

Stuffed peppers are easy to prepare and can be left to their own devices to bake in the oven. We have included Doreen's recipe here which she used to serve to her guests but, as an alternative, you can stir some cooked rice into the vegetables or simply use any of the risotto recipes on pages 42–43. You will need one pepper per person, either cut in half and deseeded or with the tops cut out and deseeded.

Preheat the oven to 170°C. Cook all the ingredients apart from the cheese in the olive oil until they are softening but not overcooked.

Rub the peppers in a little olive oil and put into an ovenproof dish. Fill each pepper with the mixture and cover with the cheese.

Bake in the oven for 30 minutes until the peppers are cooked.

1 tablespoon of olive oil

1 medium onion, finely chopped

2 cloves of garlic, finely chopped, or 1 teaspoon of garlic purée

1 courgette, finely sliced

2 sticks of celery, finely sliced

1x 400g (14oz) tin chopped tomatoes, drained

30g (1oz) grated mature Cheddar cheese per pepper

Keswick boat landings

Doreen's Nut Loaf

There is something about a nut roast that is just so 1960s and worthy – however, it is delicious for both meat eaters and vegetarians and, as it reheats very well, can be made in advance for convenience or made a few at a time and frozen. Serve with a ratatouille and new potatoes in summer or spiced red cabbage and creamy mashed potato in winter.

Preheat the oven to 170°C. Melt the butter in a saucepan and fry the onion until soft.

In a bowl, mix the nuts, carrot, breadcrumbs, herbs and add the buttery onion. Add the stock and soy sauce and mix really well.

Grease a 1lb loaf tin and press all the mixture into it.

Bake in the oven for about an hour until lightly browned. Leave to cool slightly, then turn out on to a plate to slice.

30g (1oz) butter

1 medium onion, finely diced

1 carrot, grated

110g (4oz) wholemeal breadcrumbs

220g (8oz) mixed nuts, finely chopped

1 teaspoon of mixed herbs

1 vegetable stock cube, dissolved in 150ml (¼ pint) of boiling water

1 tablespoon of soy sauce

Ratatouille

This is a classic French recipe which is so versatile – it's a great vegetable side dish with beef, lamb or chicken, yet makes a tasty lunch with a crusty baguette, especially if topped with melted cheese. You can cook a big batch as it keeps for a few days and freezes very well.

In a pan, soften the onion in the olive oil and then add the garlic and stir for a couple of minutes. Add the rest of the vegetables, tomatoes, purée and the herbs. Season with a little salt and a good grind of black pepper. Bring to the boil and then reduce the heat to minimum.

Cover the pan and simmer for 30 minutes until the vegetables are softened.

1 red or white onion, diced

1 tablespoon of olive oil

3 cloves of garlic, finely chopped

2 large courgettes, sliced into 1cm thick half moon shapes

1 red pepper, deseeded and sliced

1 yellow pepper, deseeded and sliced

1 x 400g (14oz) tin of chopped tomatoes or 4 large fresh tomatoes, chopped

1 tablespoon of tomato purée

1 tablespoon of chopped mixed fresh herbs

Salt and black pepper

Dauphinoise potatoes

Everybody's favourite potato dish! Comforting, indulgent layers of thinly sliced potatoes with cream – best in winter with good waxy potatoes such as Desiree. You must use double cream not single, or it will separate as it heats through.

Firstly, use some butter to grease an ovenproof dish.

In a pan, soften the onion in the butter, then add the garlic and stir for a couple more minutes.

Peel and very thinly slice the potatoes into crisp-like slices. Arrange a third of the potato slices in the dish and put half of the onion on top. Repeat the process again and then top with the remaining potatoes.

In a jug, stir the milk and cream, season with salt and pepper and then pour over the potatoes.

Cover with foil and put in the middle of the oven for an hour. Remove the foil, sprinkle with the cheese and return to the oven for a further half hour until the potatoes are soft and the top golden brown and bubbling.

Allow to sit for 10 minutes to set and then serve.

30g (1oz) butter

1 onion, finely diced

2 cloves of garlic, finely chopped

4 large potatoes

300ml (½ pint) milk

150ml (¼ pint) double cream

Half a teaspoon of salt and a good grind of black pepper

60g (2oz) mature Cheddar cheese, grated

Spiced red cabbage

This is a warming winter vegetable which goes with all meat dishes, casseroles and roasts alike.

Preheat the oven to 150°C. In a casserole dish over a medium heat, soften the onion in the olive oil but do not brown.

Slice the red cabbage into thin strips and chop into small pieces. Put the cabbage, apples and butter in the pan with the onion. Add the apple juice, sugar, vinegar and mixed spice. Season with a pinch of salt and a good grind of black pepper and stir well.

Bring to the boil, put the lid on and cook in the oven for about 1½ hours. The cabbage is ready when it is soft and most of the apple juice is evaporated to leave a light syrup.

1 onion, diced

1 tablespoon of olive oil

Half a red cabbage

30g (1oz) butter

2 Bramley apples, peeled and sliced

600ml (1 pint) apple juice

2 tablespoons of soft brown sugar

4 tablespoons of white wine vinegar

2 teaspoons of mixed spice

Salt and black pepper

Looking west from the Summit of High Street

Roasted vegetables

Roasted vegetables are easy to prepare, smell inviting while they cook and taste sweet and delicious on the plate. You can vary them according to what is in season or looking good on the market or at the greengrocer's. In summer courgettes and peppers are delicious with red onions (especially with roast chicken) and in winter parsnips, carrots and beetroot work really well. If cooking a leg of lamb, sit it on top of the prepared vegetables and roast in the oven – the juices run down from the lamb into the vegetables, making them irresistible.

Preheat the oven to 180°C. Prepare all the vegetables and put into a roasting tin with the shallots and garlic. Pour over the olive oil and, using your hands, mix the vegetables round the tin until they are well coated in oil. Roast in the oven for an hour until softened and browned.

4 carrots, peeled and chopped into 2cm-thick rings

1 butternut squash, peeled and chopped into 2cm cubes

2 sweet potatoes, peeled and chopped into 2cm cubes

12 shallots, peeled

4 cloves of garlic, finely diced

4 tablespoons of olive oil

Cauliflower cheese

SERVES 6

Probably Elizabeth's favourite vegetable dish – a popular one with students as it's relatively cheap to make, and the perfect accompaniment to oven-baked sausages and tomatoes.

Bring a large pan of water to the boil and then add the florets of cauliflower. Boil for 5 minutes until just tender but not soft. Drain immediately and put into an ovenproof dish.

In a pan over a medium heat, melt the butter and stir in the flour. Off the heat, gradually stir in the milk until smooth. Add the mustard and a good grind of black pepper and return to the heat. Cook until the sauce is thickened and boiling, stirring frequently to avoid it sticking to the bottom of the pan.

Remove from the heat and stir in three-quarters of the cheese. Stir until the cheese is melted and you have a smooth sauce. Pour the sauce over the cauliflower.

Sprinkle the remaining cheese over the top and bake in the oven at 180°C for 15 minutes until golden brown and bubbling.

1 medium cauliflower

30g (1oz) butter

30g (1oz) flour

450ml (¾ pint) milk

Half a teaspoon of English mustard

Black pepper

170g (6oz) mature Cheddar cheese

Carrot and parsnip mash

SERVES 6

No Christmas in Elizabeth's household is complete without this vegetable dish. You can simply mash the veg with a little butter and black pepper but this version is for a special occasion and is rather richer. It is a good recipe to make in advance and then pop in the oven for 15 minutes to reheat.

Peel the vegetables and cut into even-sized pieces. In a pan of slightly salted water, bring the vegetables to the boil and then simmer over a low heat for about 15 minutes until they are softened. Drain and allow the water to totally evaporate.

Put the vegetables in a blender with the butter, cream and black pepper. Blend until totally smooth.

Put into an ovenproof dish and sprinkle with the almonds. Bake in the oven at 180°C for 15 minutes until heated through and the almonds are golden brown.

6 carrots

3 parsnips

30g (1oz) butter

Black pepper

2 tablespoons of double cream

30g (1oz) flaked almonds

PUDDINGS

It is rumoured that there are some people who don't like pudding, but thankfully we've never met them! These days with our busy lives and often working parents, many meals are rounded off with convenient (and healthy) yoghurt, fruit or ice cream, but every special meal should have a good pud as its crowning glory. The following recipes are a selection, ranging from the quick to assemble to the more complicated and decadent but which can be prepared in advance.

Bakewell tart

SERVES 8–10

There must be hundreds of recipes for Bakewell tart – the fact that it is a combination of pastry, jam, eggs and ground almonds is as far as agreement goes. This version involves a pastry base lined with preferably homemade raspberry jam and a light almond sponge – it makes a wonderful pudding which keeps well, freezes well and tastes delicious either hot or cold. The same recipe can be used to make Maids of Honour – little individual tarts for the tea table.

Preheat the oven to 190°C. Roll out the pastry and use to line a large flan dish (25cm in diameter). Line with tinfoil and fill with dried beans or a suitably sized cake tin to hold it down. Bake in the oven for 20 minutes.

Remove foil and spread the raspberry jam on the bottom. Reduce the oven temperature to 150°C.

To make the filling, cream the margarine and sugar together until pale, light and fluffy. Stir in the eggs. Add the flour and ground almonds and stir to form a smooth mixture. Spread evenly over the jam.

Sprinkle the top with the flaked almonds and bake in the middle of the oven for about 35 minutes, until golden brown, well risen and firm to the touch.

Serve warm with cream or custard.

170g (6oz) shortcrust pastry (170g plain flour, 60g butter, 30g lard, water)

Half a jar of homemade or good-quality raspberry jam

220g (8oz) caster sugar

220g (8oz) margarine

4 eggs

140g (5oz) self-raising flour

110g (4oz) ground almonds

60g (2oz) flaked almonds

Coconut tart

This makes a lovely pudding but is equally good as a slice for tea. It is moist and light and keeps well in an airtight tin. The method and ingredients are exactly the same as for Bakewell tart, but replace the ground almonds with desiccated coconut and sprinkle with strands of coconut if you can get them or leave it plain if you are unable.

Treacle tart

SERVES 8–10

This is such an old-fashioned pudding and one that is absolutely delicious. When you take it out of the oven, the smell of syrup with a hint of lemon is so utterly inviting that you are hard pressed to let it cool down. It is lovely served hot with custard but equally good very slightly warm with whipped cream or ice cream.

Preheat the oven to 190°C. Roll out the pastry and use to line a large flan dish (25cm in diameter). Line with tinfoil and fill with dried beans or a suitably sized cake tin to hold it down. Bake in the oven for 20 minutes.

Reduce the oven temperature to 160°C. In a bowl, slightly heat the syrup to make it more runny. Put the breadcrumbs with the zest and juice of the lemon into the bowl and mix thoroughly. Put the mixture into the pastry case and bake for a further 30 minutes until golden brown and bubbling.

170g (6oz) shortcrust pastry (170g plain flour, 60g butter, 30g lard, water)

220g (8oz) golden syrup

110g (4oz) breadcrumbs

Zest and juice of a lemon

Gainsboro tart

This recipe was given to us by Amanda Bradley, who worked for Elizabeth in Humble Pie. It is a coconut-y version of flapjack in a tart – the slightly chewy, buttery topping is lovely with the fruity raspberry jam. It smells delicious when it comes out of the oven and became a much-requested pudding with regulars at the delicatessen.

Preheat the oven to 190°C. Roll out the pastry and use to line a large flan dish (25cm in diameter). Line with tinfoil and fill with dried beans or a suitably sized cake tin to hold it down. Bake in the oven for 20 minutes. Remove foil and spread the raspberry jam on the bottom. Reduce the oven temperature to 160°C.

In a pan or bowl in the microwave, gently melt the butter and syrup. Stir in the oats, coconut and almond essence if you are using. Spread the oats mixture on top of the jam.

Return to the oven and bake for a further 30 minutes until golden brown and bubbling. Serve with custard, cream or ice cream.

170g (6oz) shortcrust pastry (170g plain flour, 60g butter, 30g lard, water)

Half a jar of homemade raspberry jam

220g (8oz) butter

220g (8oz) golden syrup

170g (6oz) oats

170g (6oz) desiccated coconut

Almond essence (optional)

Apple pie (with and without cheese)

'Apple pie without cheese is like a kiss without a squeeze!' goes the anonymous saying about the tradition of eating Wensleydale cheese with apple pie (and fruit cake). Often the cheese is put as a layer in between the apples – as it doesn't melt and forms a nutty crust. A good apple pie, with crispy pastry and not-too-sweet apples, is a British pudding at its best.

In a pan over a medium heat, soften the apples slightly with a tablespoon of water (until the apples are just starting to fluff a little around the edges). Remove from the heat and stir in the sugar.

Grease a large pie dish. Cut the pastry in half and roll one half out to line the bottom of the dish. Dampen round the edge of the pastry. Pour the apple mixture into the pastry and spread out. Roll the other piece of pastry to fit the top of the pie. Firmly press around the edge of the pie to seal the top and bottom together.

Use the index and middle fingers of one hand to slightly push the edge of the pastry up away from the dish and use the index finger of your other hand to gently push the top of the pastry down between the other two fingers, creating a wave effect. Repeat this all the way round the pie. Make two 2cm-sized slits in the middle of the pastry to release any air whilst the pie cooks. Rub clean water over the top and sprinkle with a little sugar.

Bake in the bottom of the oven for about 35 minutes until the pie is golden brown.

If you are making a pie with cheese, put half of the apples into the pastry, arrange the cheese on top and then put the rest of the apples over the cheese. Finish as you would for a traditional pie.

5 large cooking apples, peeled, cored and sliced

110g (4oz) granulated sugar, plus a little for the top

280g (10oz) shortcrust pastry (280g plain flour, 90g butter, 60g lard, water)

170g (6oz) Wensleydale cheese (optional)

Blackberry and apple crunch

SERVES 4

This pudding makes a speedy alternative to a crumble and works well with any stewed fruit. In the autumn use seasonal blackberry and apple, but in summer plump, ripe apricots are perfect. The crunch topping is scrumptious. It keeps well in a sealed container for a few days, or in the freezer – just crisp it up in the oven for a few minutes.

In a pan over a medium heat, soften the apples and blackberries with a couple of tablespoons of water. When soft, remove from the heat and add the sugar. Stir well until the sugar has dissolved.

Put the breadcrumbs, sugar and butter into a frying pan and stir over a medium heat for about 10 minutes until they are sizzling, turning brown and crispy. Allow to cool completely.

For an everyday pudding, put the fruit in a large bowl and sprinkle the crumbs over the top. For a more special meal, layer the fruit and crumbs in a glass just before serving (don't prepare too far in advance or the crumbs will go soggy). Best with either clotted or whipped cream.

FOR THE BASE

3 cooking apples, peeled, cored and sliced

170g (6oz) blackberries

110g (4oz) granulated sugar

FOR THE TOPPING

110g (4oz) white breadcrumbs (about four slices)

60g (2oz) butter

60g (2oz) granulated sugar

Brioche and apricot pudding

SERVES 6–8

A light brioche loaf, with its hint of vanilla, is ideal for a bread and butter pudding, and the tang of apricots in the middle balances the sweetness perfectly. It makes a delicious pudding for Sunday lunch or an informal supper.

Preheat the oven to 160°C. Cut the bread into slices and butter them. In a buttered ovenproof dish arrange half of the slices. Spread the apricot jam over the bread and layer the rest of the slices neatly on top.

In a bowl, mix the eggs, milk, cream and sugar together and carefully pour over the bread. Allow to soak for half an hour, then sprinkle the top with demerara sugar and flaked almonds.

Bake in the middle of the oven for about 35 minutes until golden brown and risen. Serve warm with cream or ice cream.

1 brioche loaf

85g (3oz) butter, softened

Half a jar of good–quality apricot jam, or stewed and sweetened fresh apricots in season

450ml (¾ pint) milk

300ml (½ pint) double cream

85g (3oz) sugar

4 eggs

Demerara sugar and flaked almonds to decorate

Traditional rice pudding

SERVES 4

Chilly day, long walk – what could be better than an old-fashioned rice pudding? You can either oven bake it or do it on the hob, both resulting in a quite different texture. Or you can do a bit of both, starting it off on the top and finishing it in the oven – that way you get the creamy texture but with the caramelised skin on top.

Put all the ingredients in a pan, over a medium heat. Bring to the boil, stirring occasionally, and then reduce the heat to minimum.

60g (2oz) pudding rice

60g (2oz) sugar

600ml (1 pint) full-cream milk

If cooking on the hob, simmer gently, still stirring occasionally, until the pudding thickens and the rice is cooked (about 30 minutes). Serve with jam and cream.

If finishing off in the oven, simmer on the hob for 15 minutes and then transfer to a buttered ovenproof dish. You might like to stir a handful of raisins in at this stage. Bake in an oven, preheated to 160°C, for a further 30 minutes until golden brown. Serve with cream.

Richmond and its Norman castle

Egg custard with nutmeg

SERVES 8–10

You can make this without the pastry base – just bake in a buttered, ovenproof dish at 150°C for about 20 minutes until set – but an egg custard is just not the same without the extra calories. A good egg custard is not too sweet, creamily smooth and topped with a sprinkling of slightly bitter nutmeg. The trick is to have a really carefully made pastry case with no holes or splits and to bake it gently to set not cook the custard.

Preheat the oven to 190°C. Roll out the pastry and use to line a large flan dish (25cm in diameter). Line with tinfoil and fill with dried beans or a suitably sized cake tin to hold it down. Bake in the oven for 20 minutes. Reduce the oven temperature to 150°C.

Heat the milk to boiling point, either on the hob or in the microwave.

In a bowl, mix the eggs and sugar together and then slowly add the hot milk, whisking all the time. Sieve the custard mixture into the pastry case. Grate nutmeg lightly all over the top of the tart.

Carefully transfer the tart to the middle of the oven and bake for about 30 minutes until set.

Serve either warm or cold with cream or fresh raspberries.

170g (6oz) shortcrust pastry (170g plain flour, 60g butter, 30g lard, water)

750ml (1¼ pints) whole milk

5 free-range eggs

85g (3oz) sugar

Whole nutmeg

Chocolate roulade

A chocolate roulade is a classic and graced many a dinner-party table in the 1990s. It goes well with berries, either rolled with the cream or served separately. It is also delicious with a slightly warm chocolate ganache sauce. The secret of a good roulade is that it stays moist, so be careful not to overcook it and then cool as described.

Preheat the oven to 160°C. Grease a 30cm x 20cm baking tray and line with parchment paper.

Melt the chocolate in a bowl placed over a pan of simmering water (make sure the bottom of the bowl does not touch the water or the chocolate may burn). In another bowl, whisk the egg yolks with the caster sugar until they are very pale and thick.

Whisk the egg whites in a clean bowl to soft-peak stage. Now stir the melted chocolate into the pale yolk mixture and, when it is mixed in, add a spoonful of the egg whites, to soften the mixture. Now put the chocolate mixture into the egg whites and fold in as carefully as you can. Pour the mixture into the tin and spread it out.

Bake in the oven for about 30 minutes until well risen, with a light crust. Remove from the oven, leave it in the tin and cover with a piece of parchment paper then a clean tea towel.

When it is cool, carefully tip the roulade over on to the paper, remove the parchment from the back of the roulade and then tip it back again on to a clean piece of parchment. Spread the whipped cream all over the roulade. Place the fruit on the cream, if required. Now carefully roll the cake, starting with the long side, until you have a Swiss roll shape.

Just before serving, dust with icing sugar and a little cluster of berries in the middle.

280g (10oz) dark chocolate

8 eggs, separated

110g (4oz) caster sugar

300ml (½ pint) double cream, whipped

220g (8oz) mixed berries (raspberries, strawberries, blueberries)

Plain meringues

Traditionally you would sandwich meringues together with whipped cream but do not prepare them too far in advance as the moisture from the cream will cause them to go soft. They are very good sandwiched together using the chocolate cream mixture from the Gateau Diane on page 176, which does not affect the crispness of the meringue.

Preheat the oven to 100°C. Using an electric whisk or food mixer, whisk the egg whites until firm. Add the sugar a little at a time until you have a smooth glossy mixture.

4 egg whites

220g (8oz) caster sugar

Line a baking tray with parchment paper. You can use a piping bag with a star nozzle or a teaspoon or dessertspoon, depending how big you want the meringues to be.

Use two spoons of the same size. Take one spoonful of mixture and scrape it on to the baking tray using the edge of the other spoon. Leave a small distance between each meringue as they will expand very slightly.

Bake in the oven for 1½ hours for small ones or 2 hours for larger ones. They will keep in an airtight container for a week.

Buttermere Valley from Honister Pass

STAMFREY FARM ORGANICS

Even a cookery book gets a love story! Sue Gaudie was living in Cornwall and was an active member of the Young Farmers. She went to Stoneleigh, Warwickshire to give a talk about her experiences of a trip to Canada and there met Angus, the son of a dairy farmer from North Yorkshire. It must have been true love to survive the distance and, in 1990, she moved up north to get married.

Clotted cream was the product that reminded her of home and was the most requested gift from visiting friends and relatives. One of those friends was responsible for the unintentional diversification of the farm near Northallerton. One day he turned up with a separator saying that, as they lived on a dairy farm, could they not make their own clotted cream. In 1999, Stamfrey Farm clotted cream was born.

Sue started off making 20 litres of cream a week but now produces over 8½ tonnes per year. When you taste the cream, you can see why it took off straight away, with positive feedback from customers and particularly from the catering trade.

In 2001, the whole dairy herd was certified organic. As Sue's clotted-cream production grew and she could no longer feed all the by-product milk to their calves, she began to look for an additional dairy product. In 2007, she introduced natural yoghurt. This yoghurt, although low in fat, has a fresh, rich and creamy texture, making it the perfect accompaniment to fruit or granola at breakfast time.

Sue attributes the richness of the products to the fact that the milk is transferred straight from the parlour, across the yard to her dairy. Within half an hour of milking, the process of making cream and yoghurt is underway – you can't get fresher than that (or lower food miles).

The contrast of landscapes along the Coast to Coast route, and the diverse products offered from the land, is perfectly illustrated by this area. If you travel a short distance from Richmond, which marks the end of the Dales, you walk out into the gentler terrain of the Vale of Mowbray. The lower rainfall and better growing conditions give rise to much richer, lush pastures and a noticeable increase in dairy herds. West Rounton and its surrounding area has one of the highest densities of dairy herds in the country.

At a time when the dairy industry is in crisis, Stamfrey Farm is testament to someone having the courage to marry a traditional product from one end of the country to an existing way of life at the other.

Diary Cow in the rich pastures around Richmond

Homemade lemon curd and walnut meringue

SERVES 8

This pudding contrasts the crispy sweetness of meringue with the sharpness of the lemon curd perfectly. The walnuts complete a delicious taste combination. Use the egg yolks left from the meringues to make your own lemon curd. The meringues can be made well in advance and stored in an airtight container.

Preheat the oven to 100°C. Grease two large round cake tins and line with baking parchment.

Using an electric whisk or food mixer, whisk the egg whites until firm. Add the sugar a little at a time until you have a smooth glossy mixture. Fold in the walnuts. Divide the mixture equally between the tins and spread out evenly.

Bake in the oven for 2 hours, until the meringues are lightly golden brown and crisp on top. Allow to cool completely.

Whip the cream until it forms soft peaks.

Just before serving, turn one of the meringue rings upside down on the plate on which it is to be served and spread the cream on it, right to the edge. Spread the lemon curd on to the bottom of the other meringue and place it carefully, curd side down, on to the bottom ring.

Dust with icing sugar and serve within a couple of hours.

4 egg whites

220g (8oz) caster sugar

110g (4oz) walnut quarters

Half a jar of homemade lemon curd (see page 67) or good-quality farmhouse lemon curd

300ml (½ pint) double or whipping cream

Hazelnut and raspberry meringue

Both Elizabeth's parents and grandparents had good, productive gardens and eating raspberries in the warm sun is a memorable summertime experience (along with peas straight from the pod). The ground hazelnuts make the meringue soft and chewy and the raspberries with the nuts are a perfect marriage.

Preheat the oven to 140°C. Grease two large round cake tins and line with baking parchment. If you are using whole hazelnuts, grind them in a food processor or blender until smooth – do not over grind as they will start to become oily. If you are using ready-ground nuts, make sure they are well within their sell-by date as they tend to go rancid when stored.

Using an electric whisk or food mixer, whisk the egg whites until firm. Add the sugar a little at a time until you have a smooth glossy mixture. Fold in the hazelnuts. Divide the mixture equally between the tins and spread out evenly.

Bake in the oven for an hour, until the meringues are lightly golden brown and crisp on top. Allow to cool completely. Whip the cream until it forms soft peaks. Lay one of the meringue rings upside down on the plate on which it is to be served and spread the cream on it, right to the edge. Place the raspberries evenly on top of the cream, sprinkle lightly with icing sugar and place the remaining meringue right side up on top. Dust with icing sugar.

110g (4oz) hazelnuts

4 egg whites

220g (8oz) caster sugar

300ml (½ pint) double cream

220g (8oz) fresh raspberries

Fields of ripened wheat awaiting harvest

Lemon meringue pie

A classic British pudding, the lemon meringue pie has been somewhat ruined by the advent of the packet mix. The original, homemade version is a delicious confection of creamy, tangy lemon custard with light-as-air, sweet meringue, all on top of a crisp pastry – perfection!

Preheat the oven to 190°C. Roll out the pastry and use to line a large flan dish (25cm in diameter). Line with tinfoil and fill with dried beans or a suitably sized cake tin to hold it down. Bake in the oven for 20 minutes. Reduce the oven temperature to 150°C.

Put the cornflour and milk in a pan (or bowl for the microwave) and whisk until blended. Add the water, butter and sugar and stir over a medium heat until the sauce is thick. Remove from the heat and add the lemon juice and zest followed by the egg yolks. Stir together until you have a smooth custard sauce and then pour into the pastry case.

To make the meringue, put the egg whites into a clean dry bowl (preferably a food mixer) and whisk until they form soft peaks. Now add the sugar, a little at a time, until you have a glossy meringue. Spoon the mixture on to the lemon custard and roughly spread it out to cover the top.

Sprinkle the top with a teaspoon of granulated sugar and bake in the middle of the oven for 40 minutes until golden brown.

Allow to cool and serve with pouring cream.

FOR THE PIE

170g (6oz) shortcrust pastry (170g plain flour, 60g butter, 30g lard, water)

2 tablespoons of cornflour

300ml (½ pint) milk

110g (4oz) butter

300ml (½ pint) water

170g (6oz) caster sugar

Zest and juice of 3 lemons

5 egg yolks

FOR THE MERINGUE

5 egg whites

140g (5oz) caster sugar

Pavlova

This is a very simple pudding to make and really, on a beautiful summer's day, with delicious soft fruits in abundance, what better celebration of the season is there? A pavlova should be fairly crispy and golden brown on the outside but mallowy and soft within. Heaps of whipped cream and whatever fruit is at its best – strawberries, raspberries, blueberries, cherries, peaches – all work well to contrast the sweetness of the meringue and they look so gorgeous.

Preheat the oven to 140°C. Line a large flat baking sheet with parchment paper and lightly draw a circle the same size as a large flan dish (about 25cm in diameter).

Put the egg whites in a clean, dry bowl or food mixer with a whisk attachment. Whisk the egg whites until they are stiff and then add the sugar, a little at a time, until you have a glossy meringue mixture forming soft peaks. Fold in the cornflour and vinegar.

Put half of the mixture on to the paper and spread it out to the edge of the circle. Using a spoon, put the rest of the mixture around the edge of the circle to form a raised lip of meringue.

Bake in the middle of the oven for about 50 minutes until the meringue is lightly brown and crispy. Remove from the oven and allow to cool completely.

Transfer to the plate on which you are serving the finished pudding and fill with the whipped cream and then the fruit. Sprinkle lightly with icing sugar.

4 egg whites

220g (6oz) caster sugar

1 teaspoon of cornflour

1 teaspoon of white wine vinegar

300ml (1 pint) double cream, whipped

450g (1lb) soft fresh fruit

Gateau Diane

When Elizabeth was a child, no family do was complete without a centrepiece Gateau Diane – an utterly indulgent confection of chocolate and meringue, it was adored and always requested by adults and children alike. It's a good alternative pud on Christmas Day, made in the shape of a Yule log instead of a round. It freezes well, so if you are in a holiday cottage and having a celebration whilst away, it is the perfect treat. It is not a difficult recipe, but you do get left with a lot of egg yolks, so why not make some lemon curd at the same time?

Using an electric whisk, whisk the egg whites until firm. Add the sugar a little at a time until you have a smooth meringue. Lightly oil and line three cake tins with parchment paper and separate the meringue mixture between them. With a palette knife, smooth the top of the meringues and put in the oven at 100°C for 2 hours.

While the meringues are cooling, melt the chocolate and butter together, either in a bowl over a pan of simmering water or in the microwave. Set to one side to cool and thicken. Using an electric whisk, put the egg whites and icing sugar in a bowl and beat thoroughly until you have a thick, smooth mixture (takes about 8 minutes).

When the chocolate mixture is thickened, spoon it into the sugar mixture and thoroughly combine. Place one meringue on a large plate and spoon a quarter of the chocolate cream on to it. Spread out evenly to the very edge and place the second meringue on top. Repeat for the second and third meringue. Using the last quarter of chocolate cream, totally cover the sides so that you cannot see any meringue.

Decorate with chocolate curls and serve with whipped cream.

FOR THE MERINGUES

4 egg whites

220g (8oz) caster sugar

FOR THE CHOCOLATE CREAM

170g (6oz) good-quality dark chocolate

110g (4oz) butter, softened

4 egg whites

220g (8oz) icing sugar

Crème patisserie tart

This is the essence of summer and a reminder of France. However, the little tarts in France so often look irresistible but are rather disappointing in reality – this will live up to its looks! In the height of summer it is hard to decide which is the best fruit – strawberries or raspberries? For this tart you can use either or both – pile them up with blueberries and cherries for a real treat. We make a sweet, buttery pastry for the base but ordinary shortcrust would do perfectly well.

Preheat the oven to 190°C. Roll out the pastry and use to line a large flan dish (25cm in diameter). Line with tinfoil and fill with dried beans or a suitably sized cake tin to hold it down. Bake in the oven for 20 minutes until lightly brown.

While the pastry case is cooking, make the sauce. In a pan, heat the milk up to just below boiling point and then remove from the heat. In a bowl (or food mixer with a balloon whisk) mix the egg yolks and sugar together until pale. Add a little bit of the milk and then add the flours, beating thoroughly. Slowly add the rest of the milk until you have a smooth mixture. Put the mixture back in the pan and return to the heat. Whisk continuously while the milk returns to the boil and the sauce thickens. Remove from the heat and add a few drops of vanilla essence. Put the lid on the pan and allow to cool completely.

When cold, put the sauce in a food processor (or whisk with a hand mixer) until it is totally smooth. In a large bowl, whisk the cream and then fold in the sauce.

Pour the sauce into the pastry case, top with all the fruit and lightly sprinkle with icing sugar just before serving.

170g (6oz) sweet pastry (170g plain flour, 90g butter, 30g icing sugar, water)

FOR THE CRÈME PATISSERIE

600ml (1 pint) milk

4 egg yolks

110g (4oz) caster sugar

45g (1½oz) plain flour

45g (1½oz) cornflour

Vanilla essence

300ml (½ pint) double cream

Berries to decorate: strawberries, raspberries, blueberries, cherries

Tangy lemon tart

SERVES 10

This is definitely the most popular and frequently requested pudding in Elizabeth's house. It is so rich yet, because of the tanginess of the lemon, it is not overly filling at the end of a meal. It is easy to make and yet will seriously impress your guests. If you are going away, bake a pastry case before you depart, so that you only need the ingredients for the filling.

Preheat the oven to 190°C. Roll out the pastry and use to line a large flan dish (25cm in diameter). Line with tinfoil and fill with dried beans or a suitably sized cake tin to hold it down. Bake in the oven for 20 minutes. Remove the foil and bake for a further 5 minutes.

Reduce the oven temperature to 150°C. To make the lemon filling, stir the eggs and sugar together in a bowl, but do not whisk. Add the lemon juice and rind and stir. Finally add the cream and thoroughly combine.

Carefully pour the cream mixture into the pastry case and place in the centre of the oven for about 35 minutes until set. The tart should be gently set like a blancmange but not brown.

Allow to cool completely, dust with icing sugar and serve with fresh pouring cream.

170g (6oz) shortcrust pastry (170g plain flour, 60g butter, 30g lard, water)

340g (12oz) caster sugar

8 free-range eggs

4 large lemons, juice and rind

300ml (½ pint) double cream

The southern façade of Blencathra from Threlkeld Common

Raspberry sherry trifle

SERVES 8–10

This treat of a trifle is an airy whisked sponge, creamy custard and raspberries lightly soaked in sweet sherry – the perfect way to round off a party. When making the sponge it's worthwhile taking the trouble to sieve the flour – it needs to be really light.

Preheat the oven to 160°C. Start by making the sponge. This is certainly easiest if you have a food mixer with a balloon whisk. However, if you don't, you just need patience with an electric hand whisk.

Prepare a tray bake tin by greasing with butter and lining with parchment paper. Put the eggs and sugar into a large bowl and whisk until the mixture is very pale and thick. Now sieve the flour directly into the egg mixture and lightly fold in with a metal spoon.

Pour into the tin and bake in the middle of the oven for about 15 minutes until lightly brown and well risen. While the sponge is baking, make the custard.

When the sponge is cooked, allow to cool and then cover with the jam. Tear or cut the sponge into bite-sized pieces and arrange in the serving bowl.

Arrange the raspberries on the jammy sponge and sprinkle with the sugar. Pour the sherry evenly over the top.

Pour the custard over the sponge and raspberries while it is still warm so that it fills all the gaps. Cover the dish with clingfilm to prevent a skin forming on the custard and allow to cool.

Whip the cream and put on to the custard. Sprinkle with the almonds just before serving.

FOR THE SPONGE

4 eggs

110g (4oz) caster sugar

110g (4oz) plain flour, sieved

750ml (1½ pints) custard (made as instructed on the tin) but with 2 tablespoons of double cream added at the end

Half a jar of homemade or good-quality raspberry jam

450g (1lb) frozen raspberries (or fresh in season)

60g (2oz) sugar

150ml (¼ pint) sweet sherry

450ml (¾ pint) double cream

Lightly toasted flaked almonds to decorate

Doreen's strawberry cheesecake

Cheesecakes are a popular way to finish a meal – they are both light and rich at the same time. Doreen's version is easy to make yet looks impressive and tastes gorgeous.

First make the base by melting the butter and stirring in the biscuit crumbs. Press into the bottom of a lightly greased 20cm loose-bottomed round, deep-sided cake tin. Chill while making the filling.

Mix the cheeses in a large mixing bowl, beat in half the sugar, add the yoghurt and cream, dissolve the gelatine as instructed on the packet, and leave to cool, then add to the cheese mix.

Whisk the egg whites until stiff, then whisk in the remaining sugar. Fold gently into the cheese mix.

Chop 170g (6oz) of the strawberries and fold into the mixture, pour over the biscuit base, and chill for 4 hours or until set.

Slice the remaining strawberries in half and decorate the top.

FOR THE FILLING

250g (9oz) mascarpone cheese

200g (7oz) cream cheese

110g (4oz) caster sugar

150ml (¼ pint) Greek yoghurt

150ml (¼ pint) double cream

1 sachet gelatine

2 egg whites

FOR THE BASE

170g (6oz) digestive biscuits, crushed

85g (3oz) butter

FOR THE TOP

450g (1lb) fresh strawberries

Chocolate sponge with chocolate custard

SERVES 6

This is just a simple chocolate sponge as for chocolate cake. The chocolate custard can be varied in richness by adding more cocoa powder or stirring cream into the finished sauce. The custard is also delicious served warm poured over ice cream.

Preheat the oven to 150°C. Put the margarine and caster sugar in a bowl or mixer and beat until pale and fluffy. Break the eggs into a small bowl, add to the butter mixture and gently mix. With a spatula, bring all the mixture down from the side of the bowl and add the flour and cocoa powder. Mix well but do not overbeat.

Pour the mixture into an ovenproof dish which has been lightly greased with butter. Place in the middle of the oven for about 30 minutes, until risen in the middle and softly firm to the touch. Make the sauce while the sponge is baking. Bring the milk to the boil. In a bowl, mix the cornflour, sugar and cocoa powder together with a small amount of milk, until you have a smooth paste. Pour the milk over the chocolate mixture and whisk until smooth. Return the pan to the heat and stir continuously until the custard comes to the boil and thickens. Serve with the sponge.

FOR THE SPONGE

170g (6oz) margarine

170g (6oz) caster sugar

3 eggs

170g (6oz) self-raising flour

30g (1oz) cocoa powder

FOR THE SAUCE

600ml (1 pint) milk

60g (2oz) cornflour

60g (2oz) granulated sugar

30g (1oz) cocoa powder

River Swale at Reeth

Lemon sponge with tangy lemon curd sauce

SERVES 6

This delicious light sponge is perfectly offset by the sharpness of the lemon sauce. Serve either with thick double cream or thin creamy custard. The sauce is also delicious served warm with vanilla ice cream and sprinkled with walnuts.

Preheat the oven to 150°C. Put the margarine and caster sugar in a bowl or mixer and beat until pale and fluffy. Break the eggs into a small bowl, add to the butter mixture and gently mix. With a spatula, bring all the mixture down from the side of the bowl and add the flour and lemon zest. Mix well but do not overbeat.

Pour the mixture into an ovenproof dish which has been lightly greased with butter. Place in the middle of the oven for about 30 minutes, until risen in the middle and softly firm to the touch.

To make the sauce, put all the ingredients in a pan and melt over a low heat stirring continuously. Bring to the boil and simmer for about 3 to 5 minutes until the sauce is glossy. Serve warm poured over the sponge.

FOR THE SPONGE

170g (6oz) margarine

170g (6oz) caster sugar

3 eggs

170g (6oz) self-raising flour

Zest of a lemon

FOR THE SAUCE

Zest and juice of 1 large lemon

110g (4oz) granulated sugar

2 egg yolks or 1 large free-range egg

60g (2oz) butter

Coconut and jam sponge

SERVES 6

Definitely a favourite winter pudding – the coconut in the sponge makes it moist and the layer of homemade raspberry jam and sprinkling of coconut on top give a delicious contrast of texture and flavour.

Preheat the oven to 150°C. Put the margarine and caster sugar in a bowl or mixer and beat until pale and fluffy. Break the eggs into a small bowl, add to the butter mixture and gently mix. With a spatula, bring all the mixture down from the side of the bowl and add the flour and coconut. Mix well but do not overbeat.

170g (6oz) margarine

170g (6oz) caster sugar

3 eggs

110g (4oz) self-raising flour

85g (3oz) desiccated coconut

Half a jar of raspberry jam

60g (2oz) coconut to sprinkle on top

Pour the mixture into an ovenproof dish which has been lightly greased with butter. Place in the middle of the oven for about 30 minutes, until risen in the middle and softly firm to the touch.

Spread the jam on top of the sponge and sprinkle with the coconut. Serve with custard.

Syrup sponge

SERVES 6

Every child has to experience syrup sponge pudding – the ultimate, old-fashioned nursery pud! Ridiculously sweet and gooey but really good especially when offset with a not-too-sweet creamy custard. We have made this as a straightforward sponge and not a traditional steamed pudding, which is even more calorific.

Preheat the oven to 150°C. Put the margarine and caster sugar in a bowl or mixer and beat until pale and fluffy. Break the eggs into a small bowl, add to the butter mixture and gently mix. With a spatula, bring all the mixture down from the side of the bowl and add the flour. Mix well but do not overbeat.

170g (6oz) margarine

170g (6oz) caster sugar

3 eggs

170g (6oz) self-raising flour

170g (6oz) golden syrup

Grease an ovenproof dish and line with baking parchment. Pour the syrup into the dish and tilt until all the base is covered. Pour the sponge mixture over the syrup and spread out. Place in the middle of the oven for about 30 minutes, until risen and softly firm to the touch.

You can either serve the pudding straight from the dish or turn it out on to a plate so that the syrupy side is uppermost – be careful when turning it out as the syrup will be very hot.

Doreen's chocolate and pear sponge

SERVES 6

Chocolate and pears are a lovely combination and this pudding, with the bite of pears and light chocolate sponge, proves it perfectly.

Preheat the oven to 160°C. Grease a 22cm x 15cm ovenproof dish.

Chop the pears and place in the bottom of the dish with a little of the juice.

Cream the margarine and sugar together in a mixing bowl. Add the eggs one at a time and mix well then sieve in the flour and cocoa powder. Fold together, add the water and mix well. Pour over the pears, and bake for about an hour until set.

A large tin of pears, drained

110g (4oz) margarine

110g (4oz) caster sugar

2 eggs

110g (4oz) self-raising flour

2 teaspoons of cocoa powder

1 tablespoon warm water

Fruit crumble

SERVES 4

Fruit crumbles are very easy and quick to make and can be varied according to what fruit is in season. Apple is always a popular one, with blackberries added in the autumn, but apricot, gooseberries, rhubarb, plums and many more are equally delicious. We have given a basic crumble for this recipe, but you can vary it by replacing 60g of the flour with porridge oats, or adding nuts or seeds to the topping. You will need about 700g (1½ lb) of fruit, lightly stewed and sweetened to taste.

Preheat the oven to 160°C. Put all the ingredients in a bowl and mix together until you have a fine crumb.

Put the stewed fruit in an ovenproof dish and top with the crumble mixture. Sprinkle with a spoon of demerara sugar and some flaked almonds.

Bake in the oven for about 30 minutes until bubbling round the edges and golden brown on top.

Serve with custard, thick double cream or ice cream.

FOR A BASIC CRUMBLE TOPPING

220g (8oz) plain flour

85g (3oz) caster sugar

140g (5oz) butter

Demerara sugar and flaked almonds to decorate (optional)

Fruit cobbler

This makes a welcome alternative to a pie or crumble and is a good family pudding. It is simply stewed fruit topped with a plain scone mixture and sprinkled with sugar. It works well with most stewed fruit, although it's traditionally associated with gooseberries and rhubarb. Stew about 1kg of fruit until starting to soften, add sugar to taste and put the fruit in an ovenproof dish.

Preheat the oven to 190°C. Mix the flour, margarine and sugar together until you have a fine crumb texture. Add the egg and a little of the milk and mix together. Slowly add the rest of the milk until the mixture is combined to form a soft, but not sticky dough.

Turn the mixture out on to a floured surface and knead lightly to form a ball. Flatten the ball slightly and cut into six equally sized pieces.

Arrange on top of the fruit, brush with a little milk and sprinkle with demerara sugar.

Bake in the middle of the oven for about 20 minutes until the top is firm and golden brown. Serve with custard, thick double cream or ice cream.

FOR THE COBBLER

220g (8oz) self-raising flour

60g (2oz) caster sugar

85g (3oz) margarine or butter

1 egg

About 3–4 tablespoons of milk

Dexter cattle near Stoddah, Penrith

BLUEBELL ORGANICS

If there was one book that Pat found utterly enchanting as a child, it was *The Secret Garden* by Frances Hodgson Burnett. Bluebell Organics is a bit like that. As you leave the main road in Forcett, you could be forgiven for thinking you had taken a wrong turn as the neglected, overgrown land (not Bluebell Organics!) to one side of the lane, and the low stone cottage to the other, gives no clue to the magic that awaits through the door in the wall. The secret garden which is Bluebell Organics was the original walled kitchen garden for Forcett Hall which can be glimpsed across the lawns through the old wrought-iron gate. The gardens had been neglected for many years and were a wilderness when Katrina Palmer and Steve Parker came in 2000 with the intention of setting up a small organic market garden to supply the local area. They have transformed the gardens, saving many of the ancient apple trees in the orchard area and bringing a sense of order to the chaos, with neat rows of fruit and vegetables giving produce all year round.

When Pat first visited the gardens it was late spring. Walking through the door in the high, brick-built old wall, the tranquillity and sense of peace assaults the senses. The wall seems to cut the gardens off from all the hurly-burly of modern-day life. As it was springtime, the land was for the most part dormant with newly planted seeds, but there was a magnificent display of blossom on the fruit trees with splashes of colour from the bluebells under them, which gave Katrina the name for her business. The 70 fruit trees in the orchard provide enough fruit for all their customers but additionally enable them to produce their own pressed apple juice – there is nothing to match the intense burst of flavour in such fresh juice.

The gardens are not always such a haven for Katrina and Steve! There is plenty of work all year round to keep them busy, with very little help from modern machinery. They grow a wide range of crops, from basics such as potatoes, carrots and cabbages to seasonally available tomatoes, cucumbers and salad leaves. They also grow pumpkins, squash, brussel sprouts, kale and cauliflowers for vegetable-box customers and for the farmers' markets. Katrina also likes to experiment with more exotic things like figs, grapes and apricots in the greenhouse, aubergines and peppers in the polytunnel as well as a large crop of peaches on the south-facing wall. In addition to their organic vegetables and fruits, Katrina makes excellent jams and chutneys from the excess crop.

If there is any time to take stock and relax a little, it is January and February when the planning and ordering for the year ahead takes place. By March, planting is in full swing which goes right through to August to keep crops coming all year round. From mid June to August, planting and harvesting are going on at the same time as the constant effort to keep one step ahead of the weeds. September is the bumper harvest month, with all the crops still productive as well as the bonus of the English fruit – apples, pears, plums and peaches. The run-up to Christmas is hectic, making sure everyone gets their organic vegetables for Christmas dinner. Then there is the battle with the winter weather to deliver the veg boxes and stand freezing at farmers' markets. Maybe it is not such an idyll after all.

INDEX

Page numbers in *italic* refer to illustrations.

For
Robert Kirkbride – brother of Pat and son of Doreen Whitehead
and Susie Baker – sister of Elizabeth

Pat and Elizabeth would like to thank the following for their invaluable contribution to this book.

Doreen Whitehead and Margaret Baker – our mothers. Both superb cooks with an ingrained love of providing good food as well as welcoming and nurturing family, friends and visitors – and then passing it on to us!

Madeline Brabbs for her skillful work on the digital imaging of the food photography as well as generously sharing her natural artistic flair with patience and a sense of humour

Derry Brabbs for providing such amazing photographs and offering great advice, encouragement and friendship

The Vintage China Cupboard for supplying beautiful crockery & linens

Sarah-Jane Forder – our copy editor

Maria Charalambous for bringing it all together with such quality design

All at Frances Lincoln but particularly John Nicoll and Andrew Dunn for commissioning and developing Rambler's Rewards

Frances Lincoln Limited
4 Torriano Mews
Torriano Avenue
London NW5 2RZ
www.franceslincoln.com

Rambler's Rewards
Copyright © Frances Lincoln Limited 2010
Text copyright © Elizabeth Guy and Pat Kirkbride 2010
Photographs © Derry Brabbs 2010
First Frances Lincoln edition 2010

A catalogue record for this book is available from the British Library.

978-0-7112-3079-8

Printed and bound in China

1 2 3 4 5 6 7 8 9

Page 1 Cleveland Way sign, Urra Moors against background of Cleveland Plain
Page 2–3 Sunrise on traditional flower hay meadows near Askrigg, Wensleydale
Page 4 River Swale with rich grazing pastures flanking the river